I0128842

Léon Gautier, Digby Strangeways Wrangham, de Saint-Victor Adam

The Liturgical Poetry of Adam of Saint Victor

Vol. 2

Léon Gautier, Digby Strangeways Wrangham, de Saint-Victor Adam

The Liturgical Poetry of Adam of Saint Victor
Vol. 2

ISBN/EAN: 9783337778132

Printed in Europe, USA, Canada, Australia, Japan

Cover: Foto ©Thomas Meinert / pixelio.de

More available books at **www.hansebooks.com**

THE LITURGICAL POETRY

OF

ADAM OF ST. VICTOR.

FROM THE TEXT OF GAUTIER.

WITH TRANSLATIONS INTO ENGLISH IN THE ORIGINAL METRES
AND SHORT EXPLANATORY NOTES BY

DIGBY S. WRANGHAM, M.A.,

ST. JOHN'S COLLEGE, OXFORD,
Vicar of Darrington, Yorkshire.

VOL. II.

ARBOR SCIENTIÆ

ARBOR VITÆ

LONDON :

KEGAN PAUL, TRENCH, & CO., 1, PATERNOSTER SQUARE.
MDCCCLXXXI.

CONTENTS OF THE SECOND VOLUME.

CONTENTS.

FOR SAINTS' DAYS.

(Continued.)

XL.

S. VINCENTIUS.

XXII° JANUARII.

ECCE dies præoptata,
　Dies felix, dies grata,
　　Dies digna gaudio.
Nos hanc diem veneremur,
Et pugnantem admiremur　　　　5
　　Christum in Vincentio.

Ortu, fide, sanctitate,
Sensu, verbo, dignitate
　　Clarus et officio,
　Hic arcem diaconi,　　　　10
　Sub patris Valerii
　　Regebat imperio.

Linguæ præsul impeditæ
Deo vacat, et levitæ
　　Verbi dat officia :　　　　15
Cujus linguam sermo rectus,
Duplex quoque simplex pectus
　　Exornat scientia.

XL.

ST. VINCENT.

JANUARY 22ND.

SEE the longed-for day arriving !
 Happy day, day pleasure giving !
  Day in which we should delight !
Let us keep this day then holy,
On it Christ admiring truly,   5
  As He doth in Vincent fight.

For his birth, self-consecration,
Feeling, faith, speech, lofty station,
  And his office eminent,
   Under the paternal sway   10
   Of Valerius his day
    Of diaconate was spent.

Slow of speech, the bishop giveth
All his time to God, and leaveth
  Preaching to the deacon's share :   15
Wreathed his words are with uprightness,
And his single mind with brightness,
  Bred of double learning, fair.

Dumque fidem docet suam
Plebem Cæsaraugustanam,   20
     Comitante gratia,
Sævit in Ecclesiam,
Zelans idolatriam,
     Præsidis invidia.

Post auditam fidei constantiam,   25
Jubet ambos pertrahi Valentiam
     Sub catenis.
Nec juveni parcitur egregio,
Nec ætas attenditur ab impio
     Sancti senis.   30

Fessos ex itinere,
Pressos ferri pondere,
Tetro claudit carcere,
     Negans victualia.
Sic pro posse nocuit,   35
Nec pro voto potuit,
Quia suos aluit
     Christi providentia.

Seniorem relegat exsilio,
Juniorem reservat supplicio   40
     Præses acerbiori.

When the truth that he believeth
Sarragossa's crowd receiveth   20
    From his lips through present grace,
    Then the prefect's enmity,
    Zealous for idolatry,
Fiercely would the church abase.

When their constant faith he learns, that never
    flagged,   25
To Valentia both in fetters to be dragged
    Doth he direct.
Neither doth the wretch that noble young man spare,
Neither to the holy bishop's age doth care
    To pay respect.   30

    These men, tired with travel-pains,
    Weighed down 'neath a weight of chains,
    In a foul jail he detains,
        And all food to them denies.
    Though to hurt them he is fain,   35
    Yet his wishes are in vain,
    Since Christ's bounty doth maintain
        His own servants with supplies.

To exile by him is the old man sent,
The younger one meanwhile for punishment   40
    The prefect keeps still graver.

Equuleum perpessus et ungulam,
Vincentius conscendit craticulam
    Spiritu fortiori.

    Dum torretur, non terretur ;   45
    Christum magis confitetur,
    Nec tyrannum reveretur
        In ejus præsentia :
    Ardet vultus inhumanus,
    Hæret lingua, tremit manus,   50
    Nec se capit Datianus
        Præ cordis insania.

Inde specu martyr retruditur,
Et testulis fixus illiditur :
Multa tamen hic luce fruitur,   55
    Ab angelis visitatus.
In lectulo tandem repositus,
Ad superos transit emeritus ;
Sicque suo triumphans spiritus
    Est Principi præsentatus.   60

    Non communi sinit jure
    Virum tradi sepulturæ :
    Legi simul et naturæ
        Vim facit malitia.

What time his pain by claw and horse-rack ends,
Vincent at once the gridiron ascends
    With spirit braced and braver.

As he burneth, fears he spurneth ;   45
Even more to Christ he turneth,
Nor, though present he discerneth
    The dread tyrant, for him cares :
Datian's cruel visage gloweth,
Tongue and hand each useless groweth,   50
Till, such furious rage he showeth,
    He beside himself appears.

Into a cave then is the martyr thrown,
And, there confined, flung down on potsherds prone ;
Still he enjoys much light unto him shown,   55
    When angels bright to him appear.
At length, upon a pallet rudely cast,
He passes thence to heaven, his labours past ;
And, thus triumphant, his brave soul at last
    Is to his Prince presented there.   60

Datian no such grave alloweth,
As man's common law bestoweth :
Violence his malice doeth   `
    To what law and nature say.

In defunctum judex sævit : 65
Hinc defuncto laus accrevit.
Nam, quo vesci consuevit,
    Reformidat bestia.

En cadaver inhumatum
Corvus servat illibatum, 70
Sicque sua sceleratum
    Frustratur intentio.
        At profanus
        Datianus
        Quod consumi. 75
        Nequit humi
        Vult abscondi
        Sub profundi
    Gurgitis silentio.

Nec tenetur a molari, 80
Nec celari potest mari,
Quem nec laude singulari
Venerari voto pari
    Satagit ecclesia.
Ustulatum corpus igne 85
Terra, mari fit insigne.
Nobis, Jesu, da benigne
Ut cum sanctis te condigne
    Laudemus in patria! Amen.

'Gainst the dead the fierce judge burneth,　65
But more glory for him earneth,
For the very wild beast turneth,
　　Awe-struck, from its wonted prey.

Lo ! untouched, a raven, flying,
Keeps the corpse, unburied lying,　　　70
And, a monstrous scheme thus trying,
　　Datian faileth utterly.
　　　　But, unholy
　　　　Heathen's folly !
　　　　What earth would not,　　75
　　　　What earth could not,
　　　　Waste, is hurried
　　　　To be buried
　　In the silent depths of sea.

Millstone's weight can hold him never,　80
Ocean must her dead deliver,
Whom the church would now endeavour
With one voice of praise for ever
　　To revere especially.
For his corpse, reduced to cinder,　　85
Fire, earth, sea, illustrious render !
Jesu ! grant in mercy tender
We and all saints may Thy splendour,
　　Duly praise *at home* with Thee !　Amen.

S. VINCENTIUS.

XXII° JANUARII.

TRIUMPHALIS lux illuxit,
    Lux præclara, quæ reduxit
    Levitæ solemnium ;
Omnes ergo jocundemur
Et vincentem veneremur   5
    In Christo Vincentium.

Qui *vincentis* habet nomen
Ex re probat dignum omen
    Sui fore nominis :
Vincens terra, vincens mari   10
Quicquid potest irrogari
    Pœnæ vel formidinis.

Hic effulget ad bis tincti
Cocci instar et jacinthi,
    Cujus lumbi sunt præcincti   15
    Duplici munditia ;

XLI.

ST. VINCENT.

JANUARY 22ND.

'TIS a morn whence victory springeth !
'Tis the glorious morn, that bringeth
Back this deacon's feast-day still :
Joy we all this morn so glorious,
Honouring, in Christ victorious,   5
Vincent the invincible.

He who bears this name of glory,
Vincent, proves the omen worthy
Of that name by what he dares :
Conquering, both by land and water,   10
Torturers' sharpest modes of slaughter,
Fearful pains and painful fears.

Like the curtain, which combineth
Blue and scarlet tints, he shineth,
Round whose loins the girdle twineth   15
Of a two-fold chastity;

Hic, retortam byssum gerens,
Purpuræque palmam quærens,
Stat invictus, dira ferens
    Pro Christo supplicia.   20

Hic, hostia medullata,
Vervex pelle rubricata
    Tegens tabernaculum,
Pio serit in mœrore,
Et vitalem ex sudore   25
    Reportat manipulum.

Ad cruenta Datiani
Dei servus inhumani
    Rapitur prætoria.
Præses sanctum prece tentat,   30
Nunc exterret, nunc præsentat
    Mundana fastigia.

Miles spernens mundi florem,
Dona, preces et terrorem
    Elatæ tyrannidis,   35
Equuleo admovetur :
Quem plus torquet, plus torquetur
    Spretus tumor præsidis.

Robes of fine twined linen wearing,
For the purple's palm preparing,
Tortures dire for Christ's sake bearing,
 See him stand forth dauntlessly ! 20

He, a victim fit for offering,
One of the red rams' skins covering
 O'er the tabernacle's dome,
As he sows, true love's tears weepeth,
In the sweat of his brow reapeth, 25
 But brings with him life's sheaf home.

Dragged to Datian's blood-stained dwelling
Datian there, devoid of feeling,
 Sorely God's saint-servant tries.
First, the prefect doth implore him, 30
Threatens now, now puts before him
 This world's highest dignities.

Warrior-like, earth's glory spurning,
From the gifts, prayers, terrors, turning
 Of despotic tyranny, 35
To a horse-rack is he fastened,
Where, while chastening, more is chastened
 The despised chief's vanity.

Flamma vigens, ardens lectus,
Lictor cœdens, sal injectus   40
     In nudata viscera,
Simul torrent, simul angunt,
Nec athletam lætum frangunt
     Tot pœnarum genera.

Antro clausum testa pungit,   45
Membra scindit et disjungit;
Sed confortat et perungit
     Cœlestis jocunditas :
Illic onus in honorem,
Cæcus carcer in splendorem,   50
Florum transit in dulcorem
     Testarum asperitas.

Collocatur molli thoro,
Sursum spirat, et canoro
Angelorum septus choro,   55
     Cœlo reddit spiritum :
Feris dato custos datur,
Mari mersus non celatur,
Sed hunc digne veneratur
     Mundus sibi redditum.   60

Claruerunt ita dignis
Elementa cuncta signis,
Aqua, tellus, aer, ignis
     In ejus victoria ;

Red-hot bed o'er flames erected,
Lictor's stroke, or salt injected   40
    Into inward parts laid bare,
Burn and torture all together,
Yet, with all their torments, neither
    Drives this champion to despair.

Prison-bound, his limbs are riven   45
By sharp sherds into them driven ;
But a brightness, sent from heaven,
    Soothes and heals him with its smiles :
There high honour his burden seemeth,
That dark cell with glory beameth,   50
And as sweet as flowers he deemeth
    Those sharp edges of the tiles.

When they to a soft couch move him,
He revives, and, as above him
Angels' tuneful notes approve him,   55
    Yields his spirit to the Lord.
Thrown to wild beasts, help is shown him ;
Ocean's billows cannot drown him ;
But men with due honour crown him,
    To his mother-earth restored.   60

Every element thus shineth,
And with fitting signs combineth,
In the victory this man winneth,
    Fire and water, earth and air !

Summe testis veritatis,   65
Ora Christum, ut peccatis
Nos emundet, et mundatis
    Vera præstet gaudia,
Ut cantemus, claritatis
    Cohæredes: Alleluia !   70

Saint, best proof of truth supplying !   65
Pray thou Christ, that, purifying
Us from sin, true joys undying
   For the pure He will prepare,
That we may, with heaven's host vying,
   In their alleluias share !   70

XLII.

S. VINCENTIUS.

XXII° JANUARII.

M ARTYRIS egregii,
   Triumphos Vincentii
Celebret Ecclesia !
Qui certanti præfuit,
Vires, arma præbuit,   5
   Regi laus et gloria !

Hic, ætate viridis,
Datiani præsidis
   Currit ad prætoria ;
Verbum verbo redditur,   10
De fide conseritur
   Grandis controversia.

" Nil," ait Vincentius,
" Fide nostra verius :
   " Ego sum Christicola :   15
" Deum verum astruo :
" Deos, præses, respuo,
   " Non deos, sed idola.

XLII.

ST. VINCENT.

JANUARY 22ND.

L ET the whole Church celebrate,—
  Triumphs of a martyr great !—
Vincent's victories to-day !
To the King, who, whilst he fought,
Help, strength, armour, to him brought,   5
  Praise and glory let us pay !

He, while still but young in years,
At the judgment-seat appears
  Of the prefect Datian :
Word for word he gives again ;   10
A grand controversy then,
  Touching points of faith, began.

"There is nothing," Vincent saith,
"Truer than our holy faith :
  "Christ I worship, Christ alone: 15
"Sire ! the true God I declare,
"And reject those gods, which are
  "No true gods, but wood and stone.

" Te minantem rideo,
" Te parcentem doleo   20
   " Sævitorque lania."
Præses, ira tumidus,
Tanquam fera rabidus,
   Intendit supplicia.

Torquet in equuleo   25
Sublimatum ferreo
   Pœna sub diutina ;
Rapit ab equuleo
Stridens igne flammeo
   Candens ferri machina.   30

Raptus a patibulo,
Clauditur ergastulo
   Testæ super fragmina :
Testarum asperitas
Florum fit suavitas ;   35
   Cœlo datur anima.

Bestiis exponitur ;
Vident, stupent : figitur
   Alitis custodia.
Mari nautæ dederant :   40
Perdito tripudiant,
   Sed jam tenet littora.

" I despise thine every threat,
" And thy mercy should regret;   20
    " Therefore, torturer ! rend and tear ! "
Then the prefect, big with wrath,
Fierce as wild beast in the path,
    Cruel tortures doth prepare.

He, upon the iron horse   25
Lifting him without remorse,
    Racks him with long-lasting pain,
Till an iron heated frame,
Hissing with devouring flame,
    Tears him from the rack again.   30

From its crossbars taken down,
Into prison is he thrown
    On some potsherds' broken ends :
Whose sharp points to him appear
Sweetness with sweet flowers to share,   35
    Till his soul to heaven ascends.

Forth to wild beasts is he cast ;
They behold ; they stand aghast ;
    By a bird is he watched o'er :
Sailors plunged him in the deep ;   40
At his loss for joy they leap,
    But his corpse now reaches shore.

Sic ubique victor est,
Cœlo, terra potens est :
    Gaudeat Ecclesia !   45
Dies est victoriæ,
Dies est lætitiæ,
    Nobis dans solemnia.

Tuo, martyr, sanguine,
Culpas nostras ablue,   50
    Reddens prima gaudia.
Ut, mundati sordibus,
Cum electis omnibus
    Lætemur in gloria !   Amen.

Thus, victorious every way,
Heaven and earth his power obey:
    Let the Church rejoice and sing!   45
'Tis a day of victory,
'Tis a day of jubilee,
    Which this feast to us doth bring.

Martyr! in thy blood, we pray,
Wash thou all our sins away,   50
    And primæval joys restore;
That, thus cleansed from sin's alloy,
We may in thy glory joy
    With all saints for evermore!   Amen.

CONVERSIO SANCTI PAULI.

xxv° Januarii.

J UBILEMUS Salvatori
  Qui spem dedit peccatori
Consequendi veniam,
Quando Saulum increpavit
Et conversum revocavit   5
  Ad matrem Ecclesiam.

Saulus, cædis et minarum
Spirans adhuc cruentarum
  In Christi discipulos,
Impetravit ut ligaret ;   10
Et ligatos cruciaret,
  Crucifixi famulos.

Quem in via Christus stravit,
Increpatum excæcavit
  Lucis suæ radio ;   15
Qui consurgens de arena,
Manu tractus aliena,
  Clauditur hospitio.

XLIII.

THE CONVERSION OF ST. PAUL.

JANUARY 25TH.

L ET us joy, that Saviour praising,
  Hope in sinners' bosoms raising,
    That they pardon will obtain,
When He Saul severely chided,
And, converted, called and guided   5
    Back to Mother-Church again.

Saul, still threats and slaughter breathing,
With blood-thirsty purpose seething,
    'Gainst the Lord's disciples tried,
Powers obtained for apprehending,   10
And, when bound, with torture rending
    Those who served the Crucified.

As he journeyed, Jesus struck him
To the earth, and, to rebuke him,
    With His radiance made him blind ;   15
Till, once more his feet regaining,
He, a guiding hand obtaining,
    In a lodging is confined.

Flet, jejunat, orat, credit,
Baptizatur; lumen redit;   20
    In Paulum convertitur
Saulus prædo nostri gregis;
Paulus præco nostræ legis
    Sic in Paulum vertitur.

Ergo, Paule, doctor gentis,   25
Vas electum, nostræ mentis
    Tenebras illumina,
Et per tuam nobis precem
Præsta vitam, atque necem
    Æternam elimina.   Amen.   30

He laments, fasts, prays, believeth,
Is baptized, his sight receiveth ;   20
 Changed to Paul that Saul became
Who had been our flock's oppressor ;
Paul, henceforth our law's professor,
 Into Paul thus changed his name.

Therefore, Paul, the Gentiles' teacher !   25
Chosen vessel ! as our preacher,
 Light on our dark hearts outpour ;
And, for us thy prayers employing,
Life for us obtain, destroying
 Death that lasteth evermore !   Amen.   30

XLIV.

PURIFICATIO S. MARIÆ VIRGINIS.

II FEBRUARII.

TEMPLUM cordis adornemus ;
    Novo corde renovemus
      Novum senis gaudium,
Quod dum ulnis amplexatur,
Sic longævi recreatur   5
      Longum desiderium.

Stans in signum populorum,
Templum luce, laude chorum,
      Corda replens gloria,
Templo puer præsentatus,   10
Post in cruce vir oblatus,
      Pro peccatis hostia.

Hinc Salvator, hinc Maria,
Puer pius, mater pia,
      Moveant tripudium !   15
Sed cum votis perferatur
Opus lucis, quod signatur
      Luce luminarium.

XLIV.

THE PURIFICATION OF ST. MARY THE VIRGIN.

FEBRUARY 2ND

L ET us, the heart's shrine preparing
With a heart renewed be sharing
   In the old man's joy again,
Joy, which, held in his embraces,
So his long-felt heart's wish raises   5
   Once more in the long-lived man.

Set an ensign for the nations,
Shrine with light, song with laudations,
   Hearts with glory filleth He ;
Now a child for presentation,   10
When a man, a sin-oblation
   On the Cross for sin to be !

Saviour ! here, here, Mary lowly !
Holy Son and mother holy !
   Move us all to glad delight   15
By that work of light perfected,
Which we now, for prayer collected,
   Image with our tapers bright !

Verbum Patris lux est vera,
Virginalis caro cera,   20
    Christi splendens cereus;
Cor illustrat ad sophiam,
Qua virtutis rapit viam,
    Vitiis erroneus.

Christum tenens per amorem,   25
Bene juxta festi morem,
    Gestat lumen cereum,
Sicut senex Verbum Patris
Votis, strinxit pignus matris
    Brachiis corporeum.   30

Gaude, mater genitoris,
Simplex intus, munda foris,
    Carens ruga, macula;
A dilecto præelecta,
Ab electo prædilecta   35
    Deo muliercula!

Omnis decor tenebrescit,
Deformatur et horrescit
    Tuum intuentibus:
Omnis sapor amarescit,   40
Reprobatur et sordescit
    Tuum prægustantibus.

The true light the Word from heaven,
Virgin's flesh the wax, hath given   20
  To Christ's candle, bright as day,
Which to hearts that wisdom showeth,
Through which virtue's path he knoweth,
  Who by sin is led astray.

As one, love t'ward Jesus bearing,   25
In this festal custom sharing,
  Doth a waxen taper hold,
So the Father's Word supernal,
Pledge of purity maternal,
  Did old Simeon's arms enfold.   30

Joy thou, who thy Father barest !
Pure within, without the fairest !
  From all spot or wrinkle free!
Pre-elect of the Belovèd !
By the Elect of old approvèd !   35
  Darling of the Deity !

Beauty of all kinds seems clouded,
Sore defaced and horror-shrouded,
  When we see thy beauty shine :
Bitter groweth every savour,   40
Hateful and of filthy flavour,
  After we have tasted thine.

Omnis odor redolere
Non videtur, sed olere
    Tuum odorantibus :   45
Omnis amor aut deponi
Prorsus solet, aut postponi
    Tuum nutrientibus.

Decens maris luminare,
Decus matrum singulare,   50
Vera parens veritatis,
Via vitæ pietatis,
    Medicina sæculi ;
Vena vini fontis vitæ,
Sitienda cunctis rite,   55
Sano dulcis et languenti,
Salutaris fatiscenti
    Confortantis poculi !

    Fons signate
    Sanctitate,   60
    Rivos funde,
    Nos infunde ;
    Fons hortorum
    Internorum,
    Riga mentes   65
    Arescentes
Unda tui rivuli :
    Fons redundans
    Sis inundans ;

Every scent the sweetest smelling
Seems not sweet, but most repelling,
    When thy scents our nostrils fill ;   45
Love of all kinds is rejected
Instantly, or else neglected,
    Whilst thy love we cherish still.

Lovely light o'er ocean's waters !   49
Mother, peerless 'mongst earth's daughters!
Parent true of truth immortal !
Way of life to grace's portal!
    Medicine all the world to heal !
Duct of wine from life's fount bursting,
For which all men should be thirsting !   55
Sweet to those in health or sickness !
Health to all, who in sore weakness
    For its cheering draught appeal !

    Fountain duly
    Sealed as holy !   60
    Outpour for us
    Rivers o'er us :
    Fount of showers
    For hearts' flowers !
    Water ever   65
    From thy river
To all thirsting souls impart :
    Fount o'erflowing !
    Through hearts going,

II.   D

Cordis prava   70
Quæque lava ;
Fons sublimis,
Munde nimis,
Ab immundo
Munda mundo   75
Cor immundi populi.   Amen.

Grant ablution   70
From pollution :
Fountain, given
Pure from heaven !
From earth, wholly
Impure, throughly   75
Purify man's impure heart !   Amen.

XLV.
ANNUNCIATIO BEATÆ MARIÆ VIRGINIS.

xxv° Martii.

M ISSUS Gabriel de cœlis,
Verbi bajulus fidelis,
Sacris disserit loquelis
    Cum beata Virgine ;
Verbum bonum et suave   5
Pandit intus in conclave
Et ex *Eva* format *Ave*,
    Evæ verso nomine.

Metum pellit, dat solamen :
"Nam per sacrum," inquit, " Flamen 10
" Et virtutis obumbramen
    " Deo gravidaberis."
—" Mater fiam," inquit illa,
" Cujus vera sum ancilla ;
"Salva tamen sint sigilla   15
    Pudoris, ut loqueris."

Consequenter, juxta pactum,
Adest Verbum caro factum :
Semper tamen est intactum
    Puellare gremium.   20

XLV.

THE ANNUNCIATION OF THE BLESSED VIRGIN MARY.

MARCH 25TH.

G ABRIEL, sent from heaven to carry,
As Christ's faithful emissary,
Greetings to the Blessed Mary,
    Sacred words with her rehearsed:
Good and sweet the word he taketh,   5
As he in her chamber speaketh,
And of " Eva " " Ave " maketh,
    Having Eve's name thus reversed.

Comfort gives he, fear dispelling,
" By the Holy Ghost's in-dwelling,   10
" Thee the Highest's shadow veiling,
    " Thou," saith he, " shalt bear the Lord ! "
—" Be it so," by her was spoken,
" To His handmaid by this token ;
" Let my virgin seal unbroken   15
    " Be, according to thy word ! "

As that promise thus declareth,
The incarnate Word appeareth :
But the virgin ever shareth
    Still intact virginity.   20

Parem pariens ignorat,
Et, quam homo non deflorat,
Non torquetur, nec laborat,
    Quando parit filium.

Signum audis novitatis,   25
Crede solum, et est satis :
Non est tuæ facultatis
    Solvere corrigiam.
Grande signum et insigne
Est in rubo et in igne,   30
Ne appropiet indigne
    Calceatus quispiam.

Virga sicca sine rore
Novo ritu, novo more,
Fructum protulit cum flore :   35
    Sic et virgo peperit.
Benedictus talis fructus,
Fructus gaudii, non luctus !
Non erit Adam seductus
    Si de hoc gustaverit.   40

Jesus noster, Jesus bonus,
Piæ matris pium onus,
Cujus est in cœlo thronus,
    Ponitur in stabulo.

Such a birth no mother showeth;
She, whom mortal man ne'er knoweth,
Pain nor labour undergoeth,
　　When she bears her progeny.

Of a wonder new thou hearest :　　　　25
Have but faith, 'twill then be clearest :
This shoe's latchet, if thou nearest,
　　Thou art powerless to untie.
Great the lesson is, none higher !
In the bush and in the fire;　　　　30
With feet shod let none draw nigher,
　　Lest he come unworthily.

The dry rod, without a shower,
In new manner, through new power,
Fruit produced as well as flower :　　　35
　　So a maid hath borne a son !
Blessed be that fruit for ever,
Fruit of joy, of sorrow never !
Had he tasted its sweet savour,
　　Adam ne'er had been undone.　　　40

Jesus, gentle as none other,
Holy son of holy mother,
King of heaven, is, as our brother,
　　To a manger-cradle brought.

Qui sic est pro nobis natus,   45
Nostros deleat reatus,
Quia noster incolatus
    Hic est in periculo.   Amen.

May He, thus for our salvation   45
Born, effect our guilt's purgation,
Seeing that our occupation
   Of this earth with risk is fraught.   Amen.

XLVI.

ANNUNCIATIO BEATÆ MARIÆ VIRGINIS.

xxv° Martii.

PARANYMPHUS salutat virginem,
Novi partus assignans ordinem :

" En," inquit, " concipies
" Parvulumque paries,
" Nec pudoris senties   5
" Læsionem."
Jam præventa gratia,
Sed de modo dubia,
Quærit rei nescia
Rationem.   10

O Maria, ne formides;
Præbe fidem, quia fides
Potens in hoc opere.
O Maria, sis secura,
Nutu Dei paritura   15
Sine viri fœdere.

THE ANNUNCIATION OF THE BLESSED VIRGIN MARY.

MARCH 25TH.

THE bridesman thus salutes a maid on earth,
And tells the order of a wondrous birth :

" Lo !" saith he, "thou, blessed one !
"Shalt conceive and bear a son,
"Nor shalt know thy virgin zone   5
" Hath been broken ! "
Forewarned by the grace of God
Now, but doubtful of the mode,
She, since naught she understood,
   Asks a token.   10

Fear thou not, O blessed Mary !
Show thy faith, for faith can carry
   Thee through this effectually.
Care and doubt, O Mary ! still thou,
Since a mother by God's will thou,   15
   With no man allied, shalt be.

Verbum carni jungitur
Virginis in utero,
Nec natura tollitur
Unius ab altero.   20

O felix novitas !
O mira dignatio !
Contracta Deitas
Jacet in præsepio.

O Puer sapiens !   25
O Verbum vagiens !
O majestas humilis !
Nos juva, nos rege,
Nos Verbo protege,
Nobis carne similis !   30

O Maria, mater Dei,
Spe respirant in te rei,
Tu post Deum nostræ spei
Salus et fiducia.
Jesu pie, Jesu fortis,   35
Jesu nostræ dux cohortis,
Fac nos esse tuæ sortis
In gloria,
Tuæ matris gratia.   Amen.

In a virgin's womb, her Son,
    Thus the Word incarnate lay ;
But the nature of the one
    Took the other's not away.   20

    O thing most strange and blest !
Love most wonderful indeed !
    The Godhead, close compressed,
Lieth in a manger-bed !

    O Child exceeding wise !   25
    O Word that whines and cries !
        O majestic lowliness !
Both help us and direct,
And, as the Word, protect,
    Like us in our fleshly dress !   30

Mary, who thus God conceivest,
And the sinner's hopes revivest !
After God to hope thou givest
    Strength and confidence well-tried.
Jesu, mighty and endearing !   35
Jesu ! at our head appearing,
Grant we may Thy lot be sharing
    By Thy side,
Through Thy mother glorified !   Amen.

XLVII.

INVENTIO CRUCIS.

III° MAII.

L AUDES Crucis attollamus
Nos qui Crucis exultamus
Speciali gloria :
Nam in Cruce triumphamus,
Hostem ferum superamus   5
Vitali victoria.

Dulce melos
Tangat cœlos !
Dulce lignum
Dulci dignum   10
Credimus melodia :
Voci vita non discordet ;
Cum vox vitam non remordet,
Dulcis est symphonia.

Servi Crucis Crucem laudent,   15
Per quam Crucem sibi gaudent
Vitæ dari munera.

XLVII.

THE INVENTION OF THE CROSS.

MAY 3RD.

TO the Cross its due laudation
    Let us give ; our exultation
    Is its special glory bright :
'Tis the Cross our victory sendeth,
Victory sure, that never endeth,   5
    O'er our fierce foe in the fight.

    Sweet strains ! flow ye,
    Heavenward go ye !
    Since for sweetest
    Strains the meetest   10
Count we thee, sweet tree ! to be :
But let life and voice be one,
For with these in unison,
    Dulcet is the symphony.

Let its servants' praise be given   15
To the Cross, which life in Heaven,
    Joyous gift ! for them prepares :

Dicant omnes et dicant singuli :
Ave salus totius sæculi,
   Arbor salutifera !   20

O quam felix, quam præclara
Fuit hæc salutis ara,
   Rubens Agni sanguine ;
Agni sine macula,
Qui mundavit sæcula   25
   Ab antiquo crimine !

Hæc est scala peccatorum,
Per quam Christus, Rex cœlorum,
   Ad se traxit omnia ;
Forma cujus hoc ostendit   30
Quæ terrarum comprehendit
   Quatuor confinia.

Non sunt nova sacramenta,
Non recenter est inventa
   Crucis hæc religio :   35
Ista dulces aquas fecit ;
Per hanc silex aquas jecit
   Moysis officio.

Nulla salus est in domo,
Nisi cruce munit homo   40
   Superliminaria :

Yea, one and all, let them its praise rehearse :
All hail ! Salvation of the universe !
   Tree, that man's salvation bears !   20

O the blissful exaltation
Of this altar of salvation,
   Reddened with the Lamb's blood spilt !
E'en the Lamb without a stain,
Who hath cleansed the world again   25
   From the first man's sin and guilt !

Ladder this to sinners given,
By which Christ, the King of heaven,
   All things to Himself hath led ;
Whose form, rightly comprehended,   30
Shows that its four arms, extended
   Wide, o'er earth's four quarters spread.

No new mystery we mention ;
'Tis not recent the invention
   Of this doctrine of the Cross :   35
Marah's waters did it sweeten ;
And the flint, by Moses beaten
   With it, did its torrents toss.

For a house no guard availeth,
O'er whose lintel a man faileth   40
   To erect the Cross's sign :

II.   E

Neque sensit gladium,
Nec amisit filium
    Quisquis egit talia.

Ligna legens in Sarepta   45
Spem salutis est adepta
    Pauper muliercula :
    Sine lignis fidei
    Nec lecythus olei
        Valet, nec farinula.   50

        In Scripturis
        Sub figuris
        Ista latent,
        Sed jam patent
    Crucis beneficia ;   55
        Reges credunt,
        Hostes cedunt ;
        Sola cruce,
        Christo duce,
    Unus fugat millia.   60

Roma naves universas
In profundum vidit mersas
    Una cum Maxentio :
Fusi Thraces, cæsi Persæ,
Sed et partis dux adversæ,   65
    Victus ab Heraclio.

Sword ne'er smote, nor son was lost,
In the dwelling, whose door-post
    Bore aloft the mark divine.

In Sarepta, two sticks gleaning,   45
The poor widow of attaining
    Sure relief good hope did feel ;
And, without faith's sticks we use,
Nought avails the oil's small cruse,
    Nor the little store of meal.   50

    In the Scriptures,
    'Neath type-pictures,
    Lie these latent,
    But now patent,
Benefits the Cross bestows ;   55
    Faith kings cherish ;
    Foemen perish ;
    One crusader,
    Christ his leader,
Puts to flight a thousand foes.   60

Rome beheld those vessels founder,
Bridging o'er the river round her,
    And Maxentius with them drown :
Thracians flying, Persians dying,
Prone too was the foes' chief lying,   65
    By Heraclius o'erthrown.

Ista suos fortiores
Semper facit et victorcs ;
Morbos sanat et languores,
    Reprimit dæmonia ;   70
Dat captivis libertatem,
Vitæ confert novitatem,
Ad antiquam dignitatem :
    Crux reduxit omnia.

O Crux, lignum triumphale,   75
Vera mundi salus, vale !
Inter ligna nullum tale
    Fronde, flore, germine ;
Medicina Christiana,
Salva sanos, ægros sana :   80
Quod non valet vis humana
    Fit in tuo nomine.

Assistentes Crucis laudi,
Consecrator Crucis, audi,
Atque servos tuæ Crucis   85
Post hanc vitam, veræ lucis
    Transfer ad palatia ;
Quos tormento vis servire,
Fac tormenta non sentire ;
Sed quum dies erit iræ,   90
Confer nobis et largire
    Sempiterna gaudia.   Amen.

'Tis the Cross their courage waketh,
And its own victorious maketh ;
Hence disease and weakness taketh ;
    Doth the powers of hell restrain ;   70
Freedom to the captive giveth,
And new life to all that liveth ;
Yea, in everything reviveth
    Their old glory once again.

Cross ! farewell, thou tree of glory !   75
This world's true salvation's story !
Not a tree is there before thee
    Ranked for leaf or bud or flower :
Christian medicine ! health assure thou
To the whole ; the sick man cure thou :   80
In thy name, so high and pure, now
    Things are done which pass man's power.

Thou, from whom the Cross draws blessing !
Hear us now Thy praise confessing,
And, when this life here is ended,   85
Those, who on it have attended,
    In the halls of true light place.
Serving Thee, should torments try us,
Grant those torments may pass by us :
When the day of wrath draws nigh us,   90
With eternal joys supply us
    Richly of Thy bounteous grace ! Amen.

XLVIII.

IN CONVERSIONE S. AUGUSTINI.

v° Maii.

A UGUSTINI præconia
    Cuncti fideles personent !
Spiritali lætitia
    Lingua, mens, vita consonent !

Patris nostri solemnia,   5
    Quæ annuatim redeunt,
Nos invitant ad gaudia
    Quæ nullo fine transeunt.

Hic instructus in artibus
Quas liberales dicimus   10
Et in Scripturis omnibus
Quibus hærebat animus.

Primo tumens inaniter
    Mundana sapientia,
Volebat sensibiliter   15
    Scire invisibilia.

XLVIII.

THE CONVERSION OF ST. AUGUSTINE.

MAY 5TH.

L ET all the faithful tell around
Augustine's praises publicly;
And tongue, heart, life, together sound
In spiritual ecstasy !

Our father's solemn festal rites,   5
Returning to us year by year,
Invite us to those pure delights,
Which nevermore shall disappear.

Well-learned in all those arts was he,
Which "liberal" we account to be ;   10
And in all Scriptures equally,
From which his thoughts were never free.

At first, puffed up with earthly lore,
Which neither end nor object knew,
He wished unseen things to explore   15
By light his senses on them threw.

Adhuc vivens gentiliter,
Hoc errore decipitur,
Ut crederet veraciter
Ficum flere dum carpitur.   20

Recessit a Carthagine
Ut doceret rhetoricam :
Romæ vocabas, Domine,
Hunc ad fidem Catholicam.

Mediolanum veniens,   25
Dei nutu, non proprio,
Ambrosium inveniens,
Ejus hæsit consilio.

Post, baptismum suscipiens
A beato pontifice,   30
Mundi pompam despiciens,
Se mutavit mirifice.

Scripturæ sacræ litteris
Suum impendit studium,
Multorum legans posteris   35
Scriptorum testimonium.

Manichæis opposuit
Se murum invincibilem :
In prædicando præbuit
Se cunctis admirabilem.   40

Whilst he was still a Gentile youth,
    He falls into that error's snares,
Which would believe as very truth,
    That fig-trees, stripped of leaves, shed tears. 20

When there from Carthage he had come
    To lecture upon rhetoric,
Thou calledst him, O Lord ! at Rome
    To the true faith, the Catholic.

When, by God's will and not his own,   25
    He comes to Milan to reside,
To Ambrose there becoming known,
    He straightway takes him for his guide.

When afterwards he was baptized
    By that blest prelate, throughly he   30
The pomp of this poor world despised,
    And changed his life most wondrously.

He, whilst his studies he directs
    Towards the words of Holy Writ,
The witness for all time collects   35
    Of many a writer touching it.

He 'gainst the Manichæan sect
    Proved an insuperable wall ;
And by his preaching a respect
    Most wonderful obtained from all.   40

Ut mater ejus Monica,
Quæ venerat ex Africa,
Cognovit hoc de filio,
Exsiluit [præ] gaudio.

Nam videt quem pepererat,   45
Quem Manichæum noverat,
Morem mutasse pristinum
Et imitari Dominum.

Nos, O pater egregie,
    Tuis instantes laudibus,   50
Ab hujus mundi carie
    Tuis conserva precibus.

Jesu, dulce refugium
Ad te refugientium,
Per patris nostri meritum   55
Bonum da nobis exitum.   Amen.

When Monica his mother, who
Had come from Africa, first knew
Of the conversion of her boy,
Her heart within her leaped for joy.

For she beholds that very son,   45
Once as a Manichæan known,
Converted from his former state,
Seeking his Lord to imitate.

Illustrious pastor ! us, we pray,
    Who now thine endless praise declare, 50
From this world's ruin and decay
    Preserve thou by unceasing prayer.

Jesu ! sweet refuge, where those slake   .
Their griefs, who refuge with Thee take !
Grant us for this our father's sake   55
A good departure hence to make.   Amen.

XLIX.

SS. NEREUS ET ACHILLEUS.

xii° Maii.

CELEBREMUS victoriam
　　Nerei et Achillei,
Quos ad perhennem gloriam
　　Provexit ardor fidei !

Hi Domitillæ virginis　　　　　　　5
　　Conservabant cubiculum,
Cultores veri numinis
　　Et puritatis speculum.

Tincti fonte baptismatis
　　Per Petri ministerium,　　　　　10
Puellæ sacri dogmatis
　　Impendunt magisterium.

Horum salubri monitu
　　Rugam cavens et maculam,
Toto refutat spiritu　　　　　　　15
　　Mortalis sponsi copulam.

ST. NEREUS AND ST. ACHILLEUS.

MAY 12TH.

THE triumph let us celebrate
  Of Nereus and Achilleus now,
Whom faith's bright ardour did translate
  To endless glory from below.

Grooms of the bedchamber they both   5
  To virgin Domitilla were,
True servants of the God of truth,
  Mirrors of purity most rare.

By Peter's ministry were they
  To the pure font of baptism brought,   10
And to the maiden they display
  The precious truths that Christ had taught.

Led by the arguments they use
  Of spot or wrinkle to be ware,
With her whole soul doth she refuse   15
  The couch of mortal spouse to share.

Clementis sacris manibus
  Tecta sacro velamine,
Totis flagrat visceribus,
  Audito Christi nomine.   20

Aurelianus igitur
Domitillam prosequitur ;
Punire jam deliberat
Quam prius desponsaverat.

Succensus iræ stimulis,   25
  Ad Pontianam insulam
Cum duobus vernaculis
  Christi relegat famulam.

Ibi Priscus et Furius
  Simonis Magi complices   30
Avertebant attentius
  A sana fide simplices.

Refragantur mendacio
  Nereus et Achilleus ;
Veritatis præconio   35
  Homo cedit erroneus.

Torquetur in equuleo
Nereus cum Achilleo,
Nec extorquet Christicolis
Lictor, ut litent idolis.   40

By Clement's sacred hands arrayed
  In sacred robes, within is stirred
With fire of holy zeal this maid,
  Whene'er the name of Christ is heard. 20

Therefore Aurelian's vengeful wrath
'Gainst Domitilla breaketh forth,
And her he would before have wed
He plans to punish now instead.

As, roused by anger's sting, he raves, 25
  Christ's handmaid off by him is sent,
Together with these two, her slaves,
  To Pontia's isle in banishment.

Priscus and Furius, who were there,
  In Simon Magus' footsteps trod ; 30
Perverting with too zealous care
  The simple from sound faith in God.

Then Nereus and Achilleus both
  With arguments gainsay their lies ;
And at the preaching of the truth 35
  The pervert from his error flies.

With torture, to the horse-rack borne,
Is Nereus with Achilleus torn ;
But not a whit the lictor stirs
Christ's to be idol-worshippers. 40

Cæsi flammis sunt traditi
    Præcisisque capitibus
Suo junguntur capiti
    Quod regnat in cœlestibus.

Horum juvemur meritis   45
    Ac prece saluberrima,
Ut in compage capitis
    Membra simus vel ultima.

Nos Domitilla Flavia
    Pari juvet instantia,   50
Quæ viris par victoria
    Pari congaudet gloria !   Amen.

Flames with their mangled limbs are fed,
  And they, beheaded here, again
Are re-united with their Head,
  Who doth in heavenly places reign.

Grant through their merits, and their prayer   45
  In efficacy unsurpassed,
Of that one Head's one body there
  We members be, though least and last.

May Domitilla Flavia be
  Our help to a like constancy,   50
Who, like to men in victory,
  Can boast their glory equally! Amen.

L.

RECEPTIO RELIQUIARUM
S. VICTORIS.

xvii° Junii.

EX radice caritatis,
  Ex affectu pietatis
   Psallat hæc ecclesia !
  Psallat corde, psallat ore,
  Et exultet in Victore   5
   Victoris familia.

  Pars istius nobis data,
  Per fideles est allata
   Ab urbe Massilia ;
  Cujus prius spiritali,   10
  Nunc ipsius corporali
   Fruimur præsentia.

  Hæc est summa gaudiorum ;
  Dilatemus animorum
   Ipsa penetralia ;   15

L.

RECEPTION OF THE RELICS OF ST. VICTOR.

JUNE 17TH.

FROM the root of true affection,
And from pious predilection,
Let this church's anthem rise !
Let both heart and lips be singing,
And let all from Victor springing   5
Joy in Victor's victories.

His remains, now to us granted,
From Marseilles have been transplanted
Hither by a faithful few ;
So that whom before in spirit   10
We possessed, we now inherit
In corporeal presence too.

'Tis our joy's full consummation ;
Let us show our exultation
From the bottom of the heart :   15

Martyris reliquiæ
Laudis et lætitiæ
   Nobis sunt materia.

Nostri cordis organum,
Nostræ carnis tympanum   20
   A se dissidentia
Harmonia temperet
Et sibi confœderet
   Pari consonantia !

Choris concinentibus,   25
Una sit in moribus
   Nostris modulatio :
Vocum dissimilium,
Morum dissidentium
   Gravis est collisio.   30

Ex diversis sonitus
Fiet incompositus,
Nisi Dei digitus
Chordas aptet primitus
   Dulci magisterio.   35
Nisi dulcor Spiritus
Cor tangat medullitus,
Nihil vocis strepitus,
Nihil sapit penitus
   Carnis exultatio.   40

For this martyr's relics raise
Matter for unceasing praise,
    And an endless joy impart.

May the organ of our soul,
And our flesh's drum, control   20
    Every strain of melody,
With themselves in discord found,
And take part in all whose sound
    Is with theirs in harmony!

As with choirs in unison,   25
Of our habits too but one
    Should the modulation be :
Voices in a different key,
Habits that no law obey,
    Gravely hinder harmony.   30

Sounds by different lips outpoured
Must discordant strains afford,
If the finger of the Lord
First attune not every chord
    With a gentle mastery.   35
If the Spirit's sweetening power
Touch the heart not to the core,
Then the voice's loudest roar,
And earth's joys in richest store,
    Will be tasteless inwardly.   40

Dulcor iste non sentitur
  In scissuris mentium,
Nec in terra reperitur
  Suave viventium.
  Hunc dulcorem sapiat   45
  Et prægustans sitiat,
  Donec plene capiat
  Unitas fidelium.

Prægustemus cordis ore,
Ut interno nos sapore   50
Revocemur ab amore
  Mundi seductorio ;
Hic est sapor salutaris,
Hic est gustus singularis,
Per quem curæ sæcularis   55
  Subrepit oblivio.

Ut hic mundus amarescat,
Odor Christi prædulcescat,
Hæc dulcedo semper crescat
  Cordis in cellario ;   60
Ubi spirat fragor talis,
Fervor crescit spiritalis,
Et fugescit temporalis
  Vitæ delectatio.

Men, with minds distracted, never
　　Feel the sweetness thence distilled ;
Neither are life's true charms ever
　　Unto us on earth revealed.
May believers *here* unite　　　　　　45
But to taste of joys so bright,
Taste, and thirst for their delight,
　　Till they *there* shall be full filled !

Let our hearts' mouth taste its flavour,
That through its internal savour　　　50
We may show no further favour
　　To this world's seductive love :
'Tis a savour salutary,
'Tis a taste extraordinary,
Which doth in oblivion bury　　　　　55
　　Earthly cares 'mongst which we move.

That the world to us be bitter,
May Christ's perfume seem still sweeter,
And this sweetness ever greater
　　Grow within our inmost hearts :　　60
Where such fragrance round us floweth,
Spiritual fervour groweth,
And for all, that earth bestoweth
　　Passingly, the love departs.

Victor, miles triumphalis,   65
Christi martyr specialis,
Nos a mundi serva malis,
Ne nos amor . . . . .
   Mergat in flagitia ;
Una voce, mente pari,   70
Nos honore singulari
Te studemus venerari ;
Dum versamur in hoc mari,
   Exhibe suffragia.

Ne permittas spe frustrari   75
Quibus potes suffragari ;
Fac nos Christo præsentari,
Ut Hunc tecum contemplari
   Possimus in gloria.
Ad honorem tuum, Christe,   80
Decantavit chorus iste
Tui laudes agonistæ,
Quo præsente nihil triste
   Nostra turbet gaudia.   Amen.

Victor, soldier now victorious !   65
Of Christ's martyrs the most glorious !
From sins here to souls injurious
Keep us, lest a love all-spurious
    Sink us in iniquity :
With one heart and voice before thee,   70
Giving thee especial glory,
Strive we honour to assure thee !
Show us favour, we implore thee,
    Whilst we travel o'er this sea !

Ne'er permit their hope's frustration,   75
Who are thine own congregation ;
Cause to Christ our presentation,
That we may by contemplation
    Now with thee His glory know.
Christ ! to Thee due honour paying,   80
Have the words we have been saying
Been Thy champion's praise portraying ;
Whilst he here with us is staying,
    Let no griefs our joys o'erthrow ! Amen.

LI.

NATIVITAS S. JOANNIS BAPTISTÆ.

XXIV° JUNII.

A D honorem tuum, Christe,
  Recolat Ecclesia
Præcursoris et Baptistæ
  Tui natalitia.

Laus est Regis in præconis   5
  Ipsius præconio,
Quem virtutum ditat donis,
  Sublimat officio.

Promittente Gabriele
  Seniori filium,   10
Hæsitavit, et loquelæ
  Perdidit officium.

Puer nascitur, novæ legis
  Novi regis
Præco, tuba, signifer.   15

LI.

THE NATIVITY OF ST. JOHN THE BAPTIST.

JUNE 24TH.

L ET the Church now in Thine honour
  Celebrate once more the feast
Of the Baptist, Thy forerunner,
 On his natal day, O Christ !

Thus we praise the King's own power 5
  In His very herald's cry,
Whom He doth with virtues dower,
  And by office magnify.

Gabriel a promise making
  To the elder of a son; 10
When he doubted, power of speaking
  Lost the unbelieving one.

Born the child is, the declarer,
  Standard-bearer,
  Trump, of law and monarch new. 15

Vox præit Verbum,
Paranymphus sponsi sponsum,
Solis ortum lucifer.

Verbo mater,
Scripto pater 20
Nomen edit parvulo,
Et soluta
Lingua muta
Patris est a vinculo.

Est cœlesti præsignatus 25
Johannes oraculo,
Et ab ipso præmonstratus
Uteri latibulo.

Quod ætate præmatura
Datur hæres, id figura 30
Quod infecunda
Diu parens, res profunda!

Contra carnis quidem jura
Johannis hæc genitura :
Talem gratia 35
Partum format, non natura.

Alvo Deum virgo claudit,
Clauso clausus hic applaudit
De ventris angustia.

A voice the Word precedes,
The bridegroom's man the bridegroom leads,
    Star of morn, the sunrise too.

    She by speaking,
    He, signs making,   20
Both his parents name their son :
    At which token
    Fetters, broken,
Off his sire's dumb tongue were thrown.

John's birth was prognosticated   25
    By a word from heaven come,
And beforehand demonstrated,
    While he yet was in the womb.

That o'er-ripened age conceiveth,
A suggestive lesson giveth ;   30
    Dark truths declareth
That long-barren womb that beareth !

'Gainst the laws of nature truly
Was this John's conception wholly :
    Such a birth must be   35
Grace's work, not nature's, solely.

In her womb a virgin-mother
Prisons God, which babe this other
    From the womb's straits doth applaud.

Agnum monstrat in aperto   40
Vox clamantis in deserto,
   Vox Verbi prænuntia.

Ardens fide, verbo lucens,
Et ad veram lucem ducens
   Multa docet millia.   45
Non lux iste, sed lucerna ;
Christus vero lux æterna,
   Lux illustrans omnia.

Cilicina tectus veste,
   Pellis cinctus strophium,   50
Cum locustis mel silvestre
   Sumpsit in edulium.

Attestante sibi Christo,
Non surrexit major isto
   Natus de muliere :   55
Sese Christus sic excepit,
Qui de carne carnem cepit
   Sine carnis opere.

   Martyr Dei
   Licet rei   60
Simus, nec idonei
   Tuæ laudi,

Openly the voice, that crieth   40
In the waste, the Lamb descrieth,
   Voice, the herald of the Word !

Bright his faith and clear his speech is,
And he many a thousand teaches,
   And doth to the true light bring.   45
He its lantern, not that light, is ;
Christ that light for ever bright is,
   Light that lighteth everything.

Camels' hair his clothing made he,
   Girded with a leathern zone ;   50
Locusts and wild honey had he
   To support his life alone.

There hath not arisen any
Greater,—on Christ's testimony,—
   Of a woman born than he :   55
Christ the one exception maketh,
In that flesh of flesh he taketh
   Without fleshly agency.

   Martyr holy !
   Through we truly   60
Guilty are ; to honour thee
   All-unworthy ;

Te laudantes
Et sperantes,
De tua clementia,   65
    Nos exaudi.   -

Tuo nobis in natale
Da promissum gaudium,
Nec nos minus triumphale
Delectet martyrium.   70

Veneramur
Et miramur
In te tot mysteria :
    Per te frui
    Christus sui   75
Nobis præsentia !   Amen.

As thy praises
Fond hope raises,
Hear us of thy clemency,　　　　65
We implore thee!

Now on this thy birthday give us
Gladness promised thence to come;
Nor of like delight deprive us
In thy laurelled martyrdom.　　　　70

While such mystery
In thy history,
Lost in wonder, we revere,
May Christ through thee
Now renew the　　　　75
Comfort of His presence here! Amen.

LII.

SS. PETRUS ET PAULUS.

XXIX° JUNII.

R OMA Petro glorietur,
    Roma Paulum veneretur
Pari reverentia :
Imo tota jocundetur,
Et jocundis occupetur   5
    Laudibus Ecclesia.

Hi sunt ejus fundamenta,
Fundatores, fulcimenta ;
    Bases, epistylia ;
Iidem saga, qui cortinæ,   10
Pelles templi jacinthinæ,
    Scyphi, spheræ, lilia.

Hi sunt nubes coruscantes,
Terram cordis irrigantes
    Nuns rore, nunc pluvia ;   15
Hi præcones novæ legis
Et ductores novi gregis
    Ad Christi præsepia.

LII.

ST. PETER AND ST. PAUL.

June 29th.

R OME ! St. Peter celebrate thou !
Rome ! St. Paul too venerate thou
With an equal reverence !
Let the church be joyful truly,
And, rejoicing in them wholly,   5
Praise them with a joy intense !

These, on whom the Church is grounded,
Founded by them, on them founded,
Are her bases and roof-props ;
Curtains and the tent above her ;   10
Those red skins that form her cover ;
And her flowers, bowls and knops.

Clouds they are, light radiating,
Human heart-soil irrigating,
Now with dew and now with rain :   15
Preachers for a new law pleading,
Leaders to Christ's safe fold leading
A new flock of Christian men.

Laborum socii
Triturant aream, 20
In spe denarii
Colentes vineam.

His ventilantibus,
Secedit palea,
Novisque frugibus 25
Implentur horrea.

Ipsi montes appellantur,
Ipsi prius illustrantur
Veri solis lumine.
Mira virtus est eorum, 30
Firmamenti vel coelorum
Designantur nomine.

Fugam morbis imperant,
Leges mortis superant,
Effugant daemonia. 35
Delent idolatriam,
Reis donant veniam,
Miseris solatia.

Laus communis est amborum,
Quum sint tamen singulorum 40
Dignitates propriae;

Together toiling, they
 Thresh out the barn-stored grain,   20
In hope that thus they may
 The vineyard's penny gain.

And, as they wield the fan,
 Away the chaff is blown,
While 'neath fresh fruits again   25
 The crowded barn-floors groan.

" Mountains " is their appellation,
Catching first illumination
 From the light of the true Sun.
Such their virtue is, that even   30
Names like " firmament " and " heaven "
 Have by it for them been won.

They the rout of sickness cause,
And, repealing grim death's laws,
 Evil spirits put to flight :   35
They destroy idolatry,
And from guilt the guilty free,
 Making sad hearts once more bright.

Both a common glory share in,
Each of them however bearing   40
 Marks of greatness all his own :

Petrus præit principatu,
Paulus pollet magistratu
  Totius Ecclesiæ.

Principatus uni datur,   45
Unitasque commendatur
  Fidei Catholicæ;
Unus cortex est granorum,
Sed et una vis multorum
  Sub eodem cortice.   50

    Romam convenerant
      Salutis nuntii,
    Ubi plus noverant
      Inesse vitii,
        Nihil medicinæ.   55
    Insistunt vitiis
      Fideles medici;
    Vitæ remediis
      Obstant phrenetici,
        Fatui doctrinæ.   60

Facta Christi mentione,
Simon Magus cum Nerone
Conturbantur hoc sermone,
  Nec cedunt Apostolis.

Peter, peerless prince, presideth
O'er the whole church ; Paul provideth
   Laws to govern it well-known.

But to one is princedom given,   45
That the true faith, never riven
   By disputes, be one as well :
Many seeds doth one shell cover,
But the strength is one moreover
   Of the many 'neath that shell.   50

   Coming to Rome, they met
      Salvation to proclaim,
   For they well knew that it
      Was full of deeds of shame,
         Yet no cure discerning.   55
   'Gainst those iniquities
      These true physicians fight,
   Whose saving remedies
      Those fools oppose with might,
         Never wisdom learning.   60

As Christ's truth they there expounded,
Nero, by their words confounded,
Simon Magus too, astounded,
   Yield not to the apostles' word.

Languor cedit, mors obedit,   65
Magus crepat, Roma credit,
Et ad vitam mundus redit,
    Reprobatis idolis.

Nero fremit sceleratus,
Magi morte desolatus,   70
Cujus error ei gratus,
    Grave præcipitium.
Bellatores præelecti
Non a fide possunt flecti ;
Sed in pugna stant erecti,   75
    Nec formidant gladium.

Petrus, hæres veræ lucis,
Fert inversus pœnam crucis,
Paulus ictum pugionis :
Nec diversæ passionis   80
    Sunt diversa præmia.
Patres summæ dignitatis,
Summo Regi conregnatis :
Vincla nostræ pravitatis
Solvat vestræ potestatis   85
    Efficax sententia.   Amen.

Weakness flieth, death's self dieth,   65
Rome believeth, Magus sigheth ;
New life earth revivifieth,
    Now its idols are abhorred.

Wicked Nero, captivated
With the doctrines Magus stated,   70
By his death now desolated,
    Mourns his dreadful headlong fall ;
But these warriors pre-elected,
Ne'er from faith's straight line deflected,
In the battle undejected   75
    Stand, whom sword can ne'er appal.

Peter, who true light enjoyeth,
On the cross, head downward, dieth ;
Paul by swordsman's stroke ; whose passion,
Though thus differing in its fashion,   80
    A reward, not differing, gains.
Fathers, highest rank attaining !
With the King of all kings reigning !
May the judgment, so sustaining,
Of your power for us be gaining   85
    A release from sinful chains !   Amen.

LIII.

SS. PETRUS ET PAULUS.

xxix° Junii.

GAUDE, Roma, caput mundi,
Primus pastor in secundi
    Laudetur victoria.
Totus mundus hilarescat
Et virtutis ardor crescat   5
    Ex Petri memoria.

Petrus sacri fax amoris,
Lux doctrinæ, sal dulcoris,
    Petrus mons justitiæ,
Petrus fons est Salvatoris,   10
Lignum fructus et odoris,
    Lignum carens carie.

Et quid Petro dices dignum?
Nullum Christi videns signum,
    Primo sub ammonitu,   15
Fugit rete, fugit ratem,
Necdum plene veritatem
    Contemplatus Spiritu.

LIII.

ST. PETER AND ST. PAUL.

JUNE 29TH.

R OME! rejoice, earth's mistress reckoned !
In the victory of the second
Praised should the first pastor be.
Joy let all the world be showing,
And its zeal for virtue growing   5
Greater in his memory.

Holy love's bright torch is Peter,
Truth's light, salt that maketh sweeter,
Mount that righteousness displays,
Well that from the Saviour welleth,   10
Fruitful tree that sweetly smelleth,
Tree that no decay decays.

How aright tell Peter's story?
Though unseen Christ's works of glory,
At the first suggestion made   15
Nets and ship at once he leaveth,
Ere the full truth he receiveth
Through the quickening Spirit's aid.

Auro carens et argento,
   Coruscat miraculis :   20
A nervorum sub momento
   Claudum solvit vinculis.

Paralysi dissolutus
   Æneas erigitur ;
Petrum præsens Dei nutus   25
   Ad votum prosequitur.

Petrus vitam dat Tabithæ
Juvenemque reddit vitæ
   Potestate libera.
Pede premit fluctus maris,   30
Et nutantem salutaris
   Illum regit dextera.

Facta Christi quæstione,
Brevi claudit sub sermone
   Fidem necessariam :   35
Hunc personam dicit unam,
Sed non tacet opportunam
   Naturæ distantiam.

Quod negando ter peccavit,
Simplex amor expiavit   40
   Et trina confessio.
   Angelus a carcere
   Petrum solvit libere
   Destinatum gladio.

Gold nor silver coin possessing,
 Bright with miracles is he,   20
Who, the lame man's nerves releasing,
 Bursts their fetters instantly.

From his palsy liberated,
 Æneas once more upright stands,
When, by Peter supplicated,   25
 God unto his prayer attends.

Life to Dorcas Peter giveth,
And a youth from death reviveth,
 With a power from limit free :
On the stormy waves he treadeth,   30
Whom the Saviour's right hand leadeth,
 When he follows falteringly.

When his faith Christ's question trieth,
In his answer he supplieth
 Briefly what must be our creed :   35
Christ the Son of God avowing,
But the fitting difference showing
 In Him as the woman's seed.

His denial, thrice repeated,
Love, love only, expiated,   40
 And confession three times made.
 'Tis an angel letteth loose
 Peter from the prison-house,
  Where he, doomed to die, was laid.

Umbra sanat hic languentes,   45
Sanat membra, sanat mentes ;
Morbus reddit impotentes,
  Medici potentia.
Petrum Simon Magus odit,
Magum Simon Petrus prodit :   50
Flebem monet ac custodit
  A Magi versutia.

Hic a petra Petrus dictus
In conflictu stat invictus,
Licet jugis sit conflictus   55
  Et gravis congressio.
Dum volare Magus quærit,
Totus ruens, totus perit,
Quem divina digne ferit
  Et condemnat ultio.   60

Nero frendit furibundus,   ⌐
  Nero plangit impium,
Nero, cujus ægre mundus
  Ferebat imperium.

Ergo Petro crux paratur   65
  A ministris scelerum ;
Crucifigi se testatur
  In hoc Christus iterum.

Weakness 'neath his shadow ceases, 45
Mind and body's health increases;
Impotent become diseases
    Through this great physician's power.
Magus hate for Peter feeleth,
Peter Magus' craft revealeth, 50
And men's hearts by preaching steeleth
    'Gainst his subtle magic lore.

From a rock his name deriving,
Peter, in fierce conflict striving,
Conquers, though, whilst he is living, 55
    Lasts the contest's struggle dire.
Magus, as aloft he flieth,
Falleth headlong down and dieth,
And, most justly stricken, lieth
    'Neath the judgment of God's ire. 60

Nero fumes infuriated,
    Nero for this monster mourns,
Nero, 'gainst whose empire hated
    All the world complaining turns.

So he Peter's cross prepareth 65
    Through his crimes' abettors then,
Whereon Christ is, Christ declareth,
    Crucified in him again.

Petro sunt oves creditæ,
Clavesque cœli traditæ ;   70
Petri præit sententia,
Ligans ac solvens omnia.

Pastoris nostri meritis
   Ac prece salutifera,
Nos a peccati debitis,   75
   Æterne pastor, libera. Amen.

To Peter's care Christ's sheep are given,
Who holds as well the keys of heaven :   70
From Peter goes that sentence forth,
Which binds and looses all on earth.

O for our shepherd's merits' sake,
   And prayers that our salvation win,
From us, Eternal Shepherd ! take   75
   Our debt to Thee for all our sin ! Amen.

LIV.

SS. PETRUS ET PAULUS.

XXIX° JUNII.

L UX est ista triumphalis
  Forma lucis æternalis
    Et exemplar gloriæ :
Dies felix, dies læta,
In quo Petrus fit athleta   5
    Solemnis victoriæ !

Hic ignotus, simplex, egens,
Quærit, hami sorte degens,
    Vivendi commercium :
Indigenti, sed fideli   10
Committuntur claves cœli,
    Pastoris officium.

Nam in mari rete locat,
Sed a mari Christus vocat
    Et vocantem sequitur :   15
Remum calcat, rete spernens ;
Navem linquit, Christum cernens,
    Cujus verbo pascitur.

LIV.

ST. PETER AND ST. PAUL.

JUNE 29TH.

THIS triumphal day returning
    Is a type of endless morning,
        Counterpart of glory bright :
'Tis a happy, glad, day truly,
When for victory great and holy   5
    Peter arms him for the fight !

Simple, poor, unknown, he seeketh,
From what he in fishing taketh,
    His sole means of livelihood :
To him are the keys of heaven—   10
A poor man but faithful—given,
    And to find Christ's flock their food.

Through the sea his nets he hauleth,
But, when from the sea Christ calleth,
    Thence he at His call is led ;   15
Quits his oar, his draw-net spurning,
Leaves his vessel, Christ discerning,
    By His word thenceforth is fed.

Novæ remus speciei
Rete novum datur ei,   20
    Forma navis alia ;
Nam fit remus cœli clavis,
Rete verbum, Petri navis
    Præsens est Ecclesia.

Quem contundunt maris fluctus,   25
Hujus mundi juges luctus,
    Terror et tristitia ;
Quæ conformat lupus agnis
Et pusilla jungens magnis
    Mactat animalia.   30

Hic est pastor sacri gregis,
Hic ,archivus summi Regis,
    Hic piscator hominum ;
Super aquas maris pergit,
Vacillantem mare mergit,   35
    Sed clamat ad Dominum.

Novum nomen promeretur
Petrus petram, dum fatetur
    Vivi Dei Filium.
Sana fides, vox fidelis,   40
Non ex carne, sed e cœlis
    Manat hoc mysterium.

He hath given to him another
Oar, a net unlike his other,   20
   And a different vessel now :
For his oar the key of heaven,
For his net God's word, is given,
   For his ship God's Church below.

'Gainst him, like the waves of ocean,   25
This world's flood of deep emotion,
   Fears and sorrows fiercely beat ;
Which gives wolves a lamb-like nature,
And, as offerings, every creature
   Brings to God, both great and small.   30

Of God's flock is he the pastor,
Steward of an heavenly master,
   And a fisherman of men :
Walking on the sea he goeth,
Sinking fast, when fear he showeth,   35
   On the Lord he calleth then.

A new name he now possesseth,
Peter ! rock ! when he confesseth
   Christ the Son of God to be.
Sound that faith is, true that teaching,   40
Not from flesh,—from heaven's self reaching !—
   Emanates this mystery.

Claves duæ Petro dantur :
Clavis una, qua librantur
    Meritorum pondera ;   45
Et secunda potestatis,
Fontem ligans libertatis,
    Iter dans ad æthera.

Ter negato quem dilexit,
Flevit, eum ut respexit   50
    Salus pœnitentium,
Et baptisans animarum
Dulcis rivus lacrymarum
    Piumque suspirium.

Quid est, homo, quod superbis ?   55
Stare putas in acerbis
    Hujus vitæ casibus.
Ne præsumas, Petrus ruit ;
Ne diffidas, Petrus luit
    Noxam jam singultibus.   60

Cum consorte mœsti thori
Justa morte mœret mori
    Ananias mentiens ;
Verbo vitæ data vita,
Surgit lecto mox Tabitha   65
    Petri manus sentiens.

Unto Peter are committed
Two keys; one for scales is fitted,
　　Wherein merits' weight to weigh :　45
One the key of power is, binding
Freedom's fount, or paths ascending
　　Opening to the realms of day.

Peter, having thrice denied Him
Whom he loved, wept, when beside Him　50
　　He looked round who healeth grief :
Cleansing is that balmy river
Of sad tears sore hearts deliver,
　　And that sigh, fond heart's relief.

Why, O man ! art thou so haughty ?　55
Think'st to stand amidst this naughty
　　World's calamities and cares ?
Ne'er presume thou ; Peter sinneth :
Ne'er despair ; since Peter winneth
　　Pardon for his guilt by tears !　60

With his wretched wife the lying
Ananias is found dying,
　　A most righteous fate is such !
Life the word of life, see ! giveth !
Tabitha at once reviveth,　65
　　When she feels St. Peter's touch.

Carcer claudit datum pœnis ;
Membra rigent in catenis,
    Herodis imperio ;
Rigor ferri emollescit,   70
Claustra patent, custos nescit,
    Misso cœli nuntio.

Mundi caput, fontem mali,
Peste plenam criminali,
Romam intrat spiritali   75
    Petrus actus gladio.
Triumphando mortis ducem,
Reddit cæcis vitæ lucem,
Et Neronis diram crucem,
    Paulo spernit socio.   80

Simon autem debacchatur,
Alta petit, præceps datur ;
Paulus ense trucidatur,
    Petrus ligno figitur ;
Sic auditor præceptorem,   85
Sic dilectus dilectorem,
Sic redemptus redemptorem
    Pœna crucis sequitur.

Nos electos de sagena,
Petre, trahe ad amœna   90
Celsa Syon, ubi cœna
    Veri Agni vivitur,

Close confined by Herod's orders
In the prison's penal borders,
  Fetters stiffening every limb ;
Soft the iron's hardness groweth,   70
Doors fly open, no man knoweth ;
  'Tis an angel sent to him !

Rome, earth's head, sin's source, chief centre
Where the plague of crime dare venture,
Rome, that Rome, doth Peter enter,   75
  By the Spirit's sword on borne ;
Since death's chieftain he o'erthroweth,
Life's light to the blind he showeth,
Treating, while Paul with him goeth,
  Nero's dreadful cross with scorn.   80

Simon, mad, an height ascended
And fell headlong ; Paul's life ended
'Neath the sword ; and, limbs extended,
  Nailed is Peter to the tree :
Thus both taught and teacher, whether   85
Lover or belovèd either,
Saviour thus and saved together,
  Share the cross's agony.

Peter ! from thy net selected,
Draw us where, with joy perfècted,   90
Sion is on high erected,
  And the true Lamb's feast is spread ;

Ubi salus, ubi quies,
Expers noctis ubi dies,
Ubi Deus homo fies,   95
    Ubi semper vivitur ! Amen.

Where is rest from this life's fever,
Where night follows daylight never,
Where in endless life for ever 95
Man shall like to God be made! Amen.

LV.

COMMEMORATIO S. PAULI.

XXX° JUNII.

CORDE, voce pulsa cœlos,
   Triumphale pange melos,
Gentium Ecclesia :
Paulus, doctor gentium,
Consummavit stadium   5
Triumphans in gloria.

Hic Benjamin adolescens,
Lupus rapax, præda vescens,
Hostis est fidelium.
Mane lupus, sed ovis vespere,   10
Post tenebras lucente sidere,
Docet Evangelium.

Hic mortis viam arripit,
Quem vitæ via corripit,
   Dum Damascum graditur ;   15
Spirat minas, sed jam credit,
Sed prostratus jam obedit,
   Sed jam vinctus ducitur.

LV.

COMMEMORATION OF ST. PAUL.

JUNE 30TH.

K NOCK with heart and voice at heaven,
Gentile Church ! for victory given
Loud triumphant pæans sing !
Paul, the Gentiles' teacher, now,
Life's course finished here below,   5
Is in glory triumphing !

He, a Benjamin, when younger,
With a fierce wolf's ravening hunger,
Hostile to believers is.
At morn a wolf, at eventide a sheep,   10
He, when a star illumes his darkness deep,
Teaches Gospel verities.

He to the way of death holds fast,
Till life's way seizes him at last,
As he to Damascus speeds ;   15
Threats he breathes, now faith avoweth ;
Prostrate now, obedience showeth ;
Whom now bound another leads.

Ad Ananiam mittitur,
Lupus ad ovem trahitur,   20
   Mens resedit effera.
Fontis subit sacramentum,
Mutat virus in pigmentum
   Unda salutifera.

Vas sacratum, vas divinum,   25
Vas propinans dulce vinum
   Doctrinalis gratiæ,
- Synagogam circuit;
Christi fidem astruit
   Prophetarum serie.   3c

Verbum crucis protestatur,
Causa crucis cruciatur,
   Mille modis moritur.
Sed perstat vivax hostia
Et invicta constantia   35
   Omnis pœna vincitur.

Segregatus docet gentes,
Mundi vincit sapientes
   Dei sapientia.
Raptus ad cœlum tertium,   40
Videt Patrem et Filium
   In una substantia.

To Ananias is he sent;
Thus to the sheep the fierce wolf went;   20
   Cruel zeal no longer burns.
Fontal rite he undergoeth ;
Water, whence salvation floweth,
   Poison into spiced wine turns.

Sacred vessel, blest of heaven,   25
Vessel, whence the sweets are given
   Of doctrinal grace's wine,
He the synagogue goes round,
And the faith of Christ doth found
   On the prophets' previous line.   30

He the Cross's word declareth,
Sufferings for its sake he shareth,
   Thousand different deaths he dies :
But still a living victim he
Abides through unquelled constancy,   35
   Victor o'er all agonies !

Set apart, to Gentiles preaching,
He the wise of this world's teaching
   Foils through wisdom from on high.
Caught up to the third heaven, his eyes   40
The Father and the Son likewise
   In one substance there descry.

Roma potens et docta Græcia
Præbet colla, discit mysteria ;
   Fides Christi proficit.   45
Crux triumphat ; Nero sævit ;
Quo docente, fides crevit,
   Paulum ense conficit.

Sic exutus carnis molem
Paulus videt verum solem,   50
   Patris unigenitum ;
Lumen videt in lumine,
Cujus vitemus numine
   Gehennalem gemitum !   Amen.

Mighty Rome and learnèd Greece in turn
Bow their necks and wondrous mysteries learn :
 Spreads the faith of Christ abroad.   45
Christ's Cross triumphs ; Nero fumeth ;
And, since faith fast waxed, he doometh
 Paul its preacher to the sword.

From him thus his flesh-load casting,
Paul the true Sun everlasting   50
 Sees, the Father's only Son :
In light he looks upon the light ;
O may we through his influence bright
 Never have in hell to groan.   Amen.

LVI.

S. MARGARETA.

xx° JULII.

TUBA Syon jocundetur
Et jocunde moduletur
Clerus in Ecclesia !
Hac in die sponsa Dei
Summæ datur requiei,   5
Summa cum lætitia.

Virgô martyr Margareta
Cœli transit ad secreta
Felici victoria :
Sic æternam promeretur   10
Mercedem, dum non terretur
Pœna transitoria.

Fit simplex ferocibus
Præda carnificibus,
Ante lupum impium   15
Ovis custos ovium.

LVI.

ST. MARGARET.

JULY 20TH.

W HILST now Sion's trump rejoices,
　　Let the clergy's measured voices
In the church sing joyfully !
For to-day a spouse of heaven
To her rest on high is given　　　　　　5
　　With supreme felicity.

Margaret, a virgin martyr,
In glad triumph her departure
　　Takes to heaven's heights far away :
Thus for ever there she shareth　　　　　10
Its rewards, since here she feareth
　　Not the tortures of a day.

She, a simple shepherdess,
As a sheep before the face
Of a wicked wolf, is made　　　　　　15
Prey for cruel butchers' blade.

Sed nec pœnis vincitur,
Blandis nec seducitur,
Librando stipendium,
Dum præfert supplicium.   20

Carcerali sub tutela,
Rogat sibi [cum] cautela
Ne subrepat corruptela
     Per fraudes carnificum ;
Sponsum supplex deprecatur,   25
Hostem fortis aspernatur :
Sic mandatum comitatur
     Utrumque dominicum.

     Extenditur,
    - Suspenditur,   30
     Educta de vinculis ;
     Exuritur,
     Perfoditur
Ignibus et virgulis.

Cruor effunditur,   35
Quo tota tegitur
     Caro virginalis :
Pudet Olybrium,
Etsi tam impium,
     Facti criminalis.   40

But no tortures break her down,
Nor by soft words is she won ;
For she weighs the wage she gains,
In preferring penal pains.   20

She, when in her prison sleeping,
Ever careful watch there keeping,
Prays that no seducer creep in
     Through those butchers' cunning fraud.
To the Bridegroom, bowed, she prayeth,   25
Boldly spurns what Satan sayeth,
And in each case thus obeyeth
     The commandment of the Lord.

          From prison brought,
          Is she stretched out,   30
     Whilst upon a rack they tie her :
          Beat black and blue,
          Nigh burnt up too,
     Is she with scourge and flames of fire.

The blood doth from her gush   35
And cover o'er the flesh
     Wholly of this virgin :
Though of such impious fame,
Olybrius feeleth shame,
     Whilst the foul crime urging.   40

In aquis mortificatur
Ut et frigus subsequatur
    Lampadum incendia.
Sed in his regeneratur
Et columbæ speculatur   45
    In jove stipendia.

Clausam sub ergastulo
Carceris in angulo
    Draco deglutivit :
Quam ut absorbuerat,   50
Signum crucis liberat
    Quo se præmunivit.

Turtur pede conculcatum
    Dæmonem virgineo
Recitavit relaxatum,   55
    Quæsita de putco.

Impetrato quod oravit,
Caput ensi subjugavit
    Viva Christi victima :
Trucidata vicit mundum   60
Simul et letum secundum,
    Cœli scandens atria.

Into water plunged, she smarteth,
As the chill that it imparteth
    Doth to burnings' heat succeed.
But, therein regenerated,
She the dove's wage contemplated   45
    In the heavens above her head.

    Lo ! a dragon, as she lay
    In her prison's inmost bay,
        Doth the maid devour ;
    But the Cross of high renown,   50
    Signed ere she was swallowed down,
        Frees her from its power.

To the devil, as she pressed him
    Underneath her virgin feet,
Spake this dove, ere she released him,   55
    When he sought her from the pit.

Time she gained for prayer, then offered
To the sword her head and suffered,
    Living victim of the Lord !
O'er the world she triumphed, dying,   60
And, the second death defying,
    To the heavenly mansions soared.

In hac, virgo, lætabundus
Gratuletur luce mundus
  Christo sine termino !   65
Turba præsens dicat læta :
" Salve, virgo Margareta,
  Martyr digna Domino !"

Cœlesti cum agmine,
Summo coram lumine,   70
Pro pœna, solamine
  Sempiterno fruere ;
Roga Sponsum, proprio
Ut Redemptor pretio
Hostis ab excidio   75
  Dignetur cruere ! Amen.

This bright day let gratulations,
Virgin ! by earth's joyful nations
 Evermore to Christ be poured ! 65
Sing, ye glad crowd now before us !
"Virgin Margaret, hail !" in chorus,
 "Martyr worthy of the Lord !"

With the heavenly company,
In the sight of light most high, 70
Thou enjoyest endlessly
 Comfort for thy pain and woe :
Of the Bridegroom ask, that He
With the price He deigned to be,
As our Saviour, us would free 75
 From destruction by the foe ! Amen.

LVII.

S. VICTOR.

xxi° Julii.

E CCE dies triumphalis !
   Gaude, turma spiritalis,
     Spiritali gaudio ;
   Mente tota sis devota
   Et per vocem fiat nota   5
     Cordis exultatio.

   Nunquam fiet cor jocundum
   Nisi prius fiat mundum
     A mundi contagio ;
   Si vis vitam, mundum vita,   10
   Prorsus in te sit sopita
     Mundi delectatio.

   Hunc in primo Victor flore,
   Immo Christus in Victore
     Sua vicit gratia ;   15
   Vicit carnem, vicit mundum,
   Vicit hostem furibundum,
     Fide vincens omnia.

ST. VICTOR.

JULY 21ST.

H OLY band ! behold, a morning
  Of full triumph is returning ;
 With a holy joy rejoice ;
Heartfelt be your adoration,
And your inward exultation   5
 Publish with uplifted voice.

Joyful can the heart be never,
Till itself from earth it sever,
 Made from its contagion free :
Would'st thou live? This world then fleeing, 10
Let the love of this world's being
 Hushed to sleep within thee be.

Victor in his youth's first flower,
Rather Christ's in-dwelling power
 By His grace, the victory won :   15
O'er the world and flesh victorious,
Vanquished he man's foe all-furious,
 Victor but by faith alone !

Invicti martyris mira victoria
Mire nos excitat ad mira gaudia :   20
Deprome jubilum, mater Ecclesia,
Laudans in milite Regis magnalia.

Christi miles indefessus,
Christianum se professus,
    Respuit stipendia ;   25
Totus tendit ad coronam,
Nec suetam vult annonam
    Ad vitæ subsidia.

Præses Asterius
Ac ejus impius   30
Cómes Eutitius
Instant immitius
    Pari malitia :
Per urbem trahitur,
Tractus suspenditur,   35
Suspensus cæditur,
Sed nulla frangitur
    Martyr injuria.

Mente læta
Stat athleta,
Carne spreta,   40
Insueta
Vincens supplicia.

Martyr invincible ! Thy wondrous victory
Wondrously moves us to wondrous felicity ;   20
Mother-church ! bringing forth songs of glad jubilee,
Praise in His soldier thy King's mighty deeds for thee !

Christ's brave soldier, never tired,
Scorns with wages to be hired,
　　As a Christian, for the strife :   25
He but to a crown aspireth,
Nor the usual pay desireth
　　To support his mortal life.

The chief Asterius
With his most impious   30
Comrade Eutitius,
Equally barbarous,
　　Treat him most cruelly :
Dragged first the streets along,
He to a rack is strung,   35
Then tortured as he hung ;
Unbroken still by wrong
　　His martyr-constancy.

Bright and tearless,
Of life careless,   40
Stands the fearless
Champion, peerless
Victor o'er pains untold !

In tormentis
Status mentis   45
Non mutatur,
Nec turbatur
Animi potentia.

Pes truncatur, quia stabat,
Nec nunc truncus aberrabat   50
A Christi vestigio ;
Pedem Christo dat securus
Christo caput oblaturus
Ejus sacrificio.

Damno pedis hilarescit,   55
Frangi pœna fides nescit ;
Sinapis sic vis excrescit
Quo major attritio.
Tortor furit in Victorem
Furor cedit in stuporem   60
Dum Victori dat vigorem
Christi visitatio.

Mola tritus pistorali,
Pœna plexus capitali,
Vitam clausit morte tali   65
Ut post mortem immortali
Frueretur bravio.

In his anguish
Never languish   45
His mind's powers,
Neither cowers
His stout heart so brave and bold.

For that stand, his foot they sever,
But yet still the maimed stump never   50
    From the path that Christ trod strayed :
Glad for Christ his foot he loseth,
Who for Christ his head too chooseth
    Shall an offering soon be made.

Joy to lose his foot he showeth ;   55
Ne'er his faith 'neath torture boweth ;
E'en as mustard stronger groweth,
    As the more its grains we bruise.
Fierce the torturer's fury burneth
'Gainst him, but to stupor turneth,   60
When he Victor's strength discerneth,
    Which Christ's presence there renews.

First beneath a mill-stone shivered,
And his head then from him severed,
He from life was so delivered,   65
As, when death its worst endeavoured,
    An immortal prize to gain.

In Victoris tui laude,
Spiritalis turma, gaude :
Corde, manu, voce plaude   70
Et triumphi diem claude
    Laudis in præconio.   Amen.

In thy Victor's high laudation
Joy, O holy congregation !
Heart, hand, voice, with acclamation   70
Close this great day's jubilation
    With a loud triumphant strain ! Amen.

LVIII.

S. VICTOR.

In Tempore Paschali.

Prefatio. Martyris Victoris laudes resonent
Christiani !

1.

MORTEM ei intulit—ferox Maximianus ;—
- bonis, velit nolit, prodest malus.
Mors et vita duello—conflixere mirando—martyr
Christi cæsus—regnat vivus.

2. "Dic, in agonia—quid vidisti, athleta ? "—
"vexillum Christi regnantis—et gloriam vidi
consolantis."
Cruciatus fortes,—miracula sunt testes ; — ad
cujus preces defuncti—suscitantur, sanantur
infirmi.

LVIII.

ST. VICTOR.

IN EASTER-TIDE.

PREFACE. Let all Christians sound the praise of the
blessed martyr Victor !

1.

M AXIMIAN the cruel hath—inflicted death
upon him,—and thus blessings, will he,
nill he, won him.
Life and death together fought—in a strife with
wonder fraught:—Christ's own martyr
slain—lives to reign.

2. "Say, in thine agony—what, O champion !
didst thou see ?" "I saw the banner of
Christ reigning,—His glory too, who soothes
complaining."
Tortures' sore distresses—with signs are his witnesses : at whose petitions dead bodies—
come to life, and—healed are infirmities.

3. Credendum est magis soli Christi Ecclesiæ quam
   impiorum genti perversæ.
   Scimus ergo te regnare cum Christo : tecum col-
   locare, Victor dux, nos dignare.   Amen.

3. Far rather should we believe Christ's Church
   alone—than a race perverse, who have
   evil done.
   Thus we know that thou dost reign now; place
   for us to gain now by thee, great Victor,
   deign thou! Amen.

LIX.

S. APOLLINARIS.

XXIII° JULII.

Laudemus Apollinarem.

Cetera desunt.

LIX.

ST. APOLLINARIS.

JULY 23RD.

The text of this hymn cannot be found.

LX.

S. JACOBUS MAJOR.

xxv° Julii.

PANGAT chorus in hac die
Novum genus melodiæ,
Clara dans præconia :
Jacobum resultat lyra,
In quo floruit tam mira   5
Meritorum copia.

Patre natus Zebedæo,
Instat mari Galilæo
Arte piscatoria.
Judaismi ficus arens   10
Nutrix ei fit et parens
In legis duritia.

Ex divinæ vocis oraculo,
Pro jubentis nutu vel oculo,
Piscatoris abjurat titulo   15
Præodorans dona perennia ;

LX.

ST. JAMES THE GREATER.

JULY 25TH.

L ET our choir in sweet laudation,
    Sounding with clear intonation,
  Chant a new-made song to-day :
'Tis with James the lyre resoundeth,
Who with merits rare aboundeth   5
  In so wonderful a way.

He and Zebedee his father
Toiled as fishermen together
  By the Sea of Galilee :
Jewry's withered fig-tree bore him,   10
And, as his stern nurse, watched o'er him
  In the Law's severity.

Hearing a voice divine God's will proclaim,
He, when Christ's nod and look commands the same,
Abjures at once the fisher's trade and name,   15
  Scenting afar eternal gifts outpoured :

Synagogam mutat Ecclesia,
Patrem Deo legemque gratia,
Transfigurans mentis industria
   Navem cruce verboque retia.   20

  Vas sincerum, granum pingue,
Bibit lac coelestis linguæ,
    Vitæ sugit ubera,
Induit Apostolatum,
Coelo capit principatum,   25
    Verbo premit æthera.

Hic in sua specie
Regem vidit gloriæ
    Vultu clarum flammeo,
Quem crucis vicinia   ` 30
Vi respersit nimia,
    Sudore sanguineo.

Hunc in coena mystica
Agni carne deica
    Christus pavit;   35
Hujus mentem coelitus
Aspirans Paraclitus
    Debriavit.

Duplicem exercens alam,
Erigit coelestem scalam   40
    Sermonis et operis,

He gives the Church the Synagogue's old place,
Changes his sire for God, the law for grace,
Transforming of set purpose in each case
    Ship to the cross and nets to God's own Word. 20

He, pure vessel ! grain most feeding !
Drinks milk from God's word proceeding,
    Sucks the breasts of life on high,
The Apostolate assumeth,
A great prince in Heaven becometh,   25
    With the word attacks the sky.

The great King of glory he
Doth in all his beauty see,
    With his visage bright as flame,
Who, when now the cross drew nigh,   30
Was in his fierce agony
    Sprinkled with a blood-sweat stream.

Him too at that mystic feast
With the Lamb's divine flesh Christ
    Fed most truly ;   35
And his soul with heavenly fire
Did the Paraclete inspire
    Fully, throughly.

He, his twain wings exercising,
Sets a ladder, heavenward rising,   40
    Of words said and actions done ;

Et rebelles Deo magos
Sensu doctrinaque vagos
    Fide jungit superis.

Dabat viva vox Hebræi   45
Sonum ut sublimus Dei,
Docens lapsus orbis rei
    Solvi pœnitentia ;
Jacobus ut torrens ignis
Fulgurat virtutum signis ;   50
Rebus vacat Deo dignis,
    Cœlis infert studia.

Hinc Herodes fervens ira
Rabieque furens dira
    Jussa dat crudelia,   55
Jubens hunc ense feriri
Et immeritum puniri
    Capitis sententia.

Sic, excocto gelu martyrii,
Apprehendit coronam bravii   60
    Jacobi prudentia,
Cujus ope fulget Ecclesia ;
Stet in fide, crescat in gratia,
    Consequatur cælorum præmia ! Amen.

And of Magians, God opposing,
Wildest thoughts and doctrines choosing,
   Makes the faith with angels' one.

By this Hebrew's voice were given   45
Wakening sounds like God's in heaven,
Teaching a lost world that even
   Its sins penitence could heal :
James like vivid lightning gloweth,
Bright with marks that virtue showeth,   50
Thought on things divine bestoweth,
   And for heaven expends his zeal.

Herod therefore, hot with passion,
Wild with direst indignation,
   Forth his cruel mandate sent,   55
Ordering him to death most dreaded,
With the sword to be beheaded,
   Who deserved no punishment.

Thus, martyrdom's fierce frost all thawed and past,
St. James's wisdom wins for him at last   60
   The crown which is the victor's prize,
Through whose assistance now the Church doth
   shine :—
May its faith stand, its grace too ne'er decline,
   But gain at last its guerdon in the skies ! Amen.

LXI.

S. GERMANUS.

xxxi° Julii.

Ecce dies attolenda.

Cetera desunt.

LXI.

ST. GERMAIN.

JULY 31ST.

The text of this hymn cannot be found.

TRANSFIGURATIO DOMINI.

vi° Augusti.

L ÆTABUNDI jubilemus,
    Ac devote celebremus
Hæc sacra solemnia ;
Ad honorem summi Dei
Hujus laudes nunc diei   5
    Personet Ecclesia.

In hac Christus die festa
Suæ dedit manifesta
    Gloriæ indicia :
Ut hoc posset enarrari,   10
Hic nos suo salutari
    Repleat et gratia !

Christus ergo, Deus fortis,
Vitæ dator, victor mortis,
    Verus sol justitiæ,   15
Quam assumpsit carnem de Virgine,
Transformatus in Thabor culmine,
    Glorificat hodie.

THE TRANSFIGURATION OF OUR LORD.

August 6th.

L ET us joy and jubilation
In devoutest celebration
  Of this sacred feast display;
To exalt the King of Heaven,
Now by all this Church be given   5
  Praise and honour to this day.

On this festal day, as witness
To us, of His glory's brightness
  Christ the plainest tokens gave;
For this story's due narration   10
All the grace of His salvation
  Fully, freely may we have!

Christ then, mighty God, Bestower
Of all life, and death's O'erthrower,
  Very Sun of Righteousness,   15
Flesh that from a Virgin He deigned to seek,
On this day transfigured on Thabor's peak,
  Doth in brightest glory dress.

II.   L

O quam felix fons bonorum !
Talis enim beatorum   20
 Erit resurrectio.
Sicut fulget sol plenus luminis,
Fulsit Dei vultus et hominis,
 Teste Evangelio.

Candor quoque sacræ vestis   25
Deitatis fuit testis
 Et futuræ gloriæ.
Mirus honor et sublimis,
Mira, Deus, tuæ nimis
 Virtus est potentiæ.   30

Cumque Christus, Verbum Dei,
Petro, natis Zebedæi
 Majestatis gloriam
Demonstraret manifeste,
Ecce vident, Luca teste,   35
 Moysen et Eliam.

Hoc habemus ex Matthæo,
Quod loquentes erant Deo
 Dei Patris filio :
Vere sanctum, vere dignum   40
Loqui Dei et benignum,
 Plenum omni gaudio.

Blessed fount of good things given !
Such to all that enter heaven   20
    Will the resurrection be.
As the sun shines when it is at its height,
So the God-man's features were shining bright,
    As we in the Gospel see.

There His sacred vesture's whiteness   25
Told of future glory's brightness,
    And of God incarnate now.
Over all Thine honour towers
Wondrously, and wondrous powers
    Doth, O God ! Thy greatness show !   30

And, when Christ, God's Word from heaven,
Proof to Peter thus had given,
    And the sons of Zebedee,
Of the greatness of His glory,
Lo ! they,—Luke attests the story,—   35
    Moses and Elias see.

Matthew gives us information
Of these holding conversation
    There with God, God's Son most high :
Very fitting, very holy,   40
Was such speech, and pleasant truly,
    Filled with full felicity.

Hujus magna laus diei,
Quæ sacratur voce Dei.
  Honor est eximius ;   45
Nubes illos obumbravit,
Et Patris vox proclamavit :
  " Hic est meus filius ! "

Hujus vocem exaudite :
Habet enim verba vitæ,   50
  Verbo potens omnia,
Hic est Christus, Rex cunctorum,
Mundi salus, lux sanctorum,
  Lux illustrans omnia !

Hic est Christus, Patris Verbum, 55
Per quem perdit jus acerbum
  Quod in nobis habuit
Hostis nequam, serpens dirus,
Qui fundendo suum virus
  Evæ, nobis nocuit.   60

Moriendo nos sanavit,
Qui surgendo reparavit
Vitam Christus et damnavit
  Mortis magisterium.
Hic est Christus, pax æterna, 65
Ima regens et superna,
Cui de cœlis vox paterna
  Confert testimonium.

'Tis a day most celebrated,
Thus by God's voice consecrated;
   High distinction hath it won !   45
See the cloud about them gather,
Hear the utterance of the Father;
   "This is My Belovèd Son !"

Hear ye all God's voice supernal;
It hath words of life eternal;   50
   O'er the world His word is king;
Christ, the Lord of all creation,
Saints' bright light and earth's salvation,
   Light that lighteth everything !

Christ, the Father's Word from heaven,   55
Who destroys the stern right given
   'Gainst us to our wicked foe,
That dire serpent, who, soul-killing
Poison into Eve instilling,
   Wounded all men here below.   60

We were healed by Christ's death for us,
While His rising did restore us
To new life, and death's power o'er us
   Thereby utterly destroy.
Christ it is, our peace supernal,   65
Lord of heaven and realms infernal,
Whom God thus His voice paternal
   To acknowledge did employ.

Cujus sono sunt turbati
Patres illi tres præfati,   70
Et in terram sunt prostrati,
   Quando vox emittitur
Surgunt tandem annuente
Sibi Christo, sed intente
Circumspectant, cum repente   75
   Solus Christus cernitur.

Volens Christus, hæc celari
Non permisit enarrari,
Donec vitæ reparator,
Hostis vitæ triumphator,   80
   Morte vita surgeret.
Hacc est dies laude digna
Qua tot sancta fiunt signa ;
Christus splendor Dei Patris,
Prece sancta suæ matris,.   85
   Nos a morte lieberet.

Tibi, Pater, tibi, Nate,
   Tibi, Sancte Spiritus,
Sit cum summa potestate
   Laus et honor debitus ! Amen.   90

Those three fathers before stated
By that voice are agitated,   70
And upon the earth prostrated,
    When comes forth its wondrous tone.
Christ at length toward them turning,
They arise, but glances yearning,
Cast around them, thus discerning   75
    Suddenly Christ left alone.

Christ desiring these things hidden,
They to tell them were forbidden,
Till, as life's restorer glorious,
Over life's dread foe victorious,   80
    Life by death should rise again.
Worthy praise the day is truly,
Whereon signs are wrought so holy !
O may Christ, his Father's splendour,
Through his mother's blest prayers render   85
    Free from death the sons of men !

Father ! Son ! to Thee in heaven,
    Holy Spirit ! unto Thee,
Praise and honour due be given,
    And supremest majesty !   Amen.   90

LXIII.

TRANSFIGURATIO DOMINI.

vi° Augusti.

In eadem specie visum.

Cetera desunt.

LXIII.

THE TRANSFIGURATION OF THE LORD.

AUGUST 6TH.

The text of this hymn cannot be found.

S. LAURENTIUS.

x° Augusti.

PRUNIS datum
   Admiremur,
Laureatum
Veneremur
Laudibus Laurentium ;   5
Veneremur
   Cum tremore,
Deprecemur
   Cum amore
Martyrem egregium.   10

Accusatus
   Non negavit ;
Sed pulsatus
Resultavit
In tubis ductilibus,   15
   Cum in pœnis
   Voto plenis

LXIV.

ST. LAWRENCE.

AUGUST 10TH.

'MID the blazing
      Conflagration,
Wondering, praising,
    Veneration
Pay we Lawrence, laurel-crowned;   5
    Awe-struck bowing,
    Venerate him;
    Our love showing,
    Supplicate him,
As a martyr most renowned.   10

    They indict him,—
    He denies not;
    When they smite him,
    He replies but
In the tone soft organs raise :   15
    'Mid flames, playing
    Round him, praying,

Exsultaret
Et sonaret
In divinis laudibus.   20

Sicut chorda musicorum
Tandem sonum dat sonorum
    Plectri ministerio ;
Sic in chely tormentorum
Melos Christi confessorum   25
    Dedit hujus tentio.

Deci, vide
Quia fide
Stat invictus
Inter ictus,   30
Minas et incendia :
Spes interna,
Vox superna
Consolantur
Et hortantur   35
Virum de constantia.

Nam thesauros quos exquiris
Per tormenta non acquiris
    Tibi, sed Laurentio.
Hos in Christo coacervat,   40
Cujus pugnam Christus servat
    Triumphantis præmio.

He rejoices,
And his voice is
Lifted to his Maker's praise.   20

As sweet sounds the harp-string waketh
And enchanting music maketh,
    Which the minstrel's light quill hits,
So the martyr's frame, extended
On the lyre of torture, blended   25
    Strains of faith and hope emits.

Decius ! see how
Brave stands he now,
As faith urges
'Neath the scourges,   30
Threats, and fierce flames mounting high ;
Hope internal,
Words supernal,
Consolation,
Exhortation,   35
Give the man to constancy.

For the treasure which thou seekest
With these tortures thou bespeakest
    For St. Lawrence, not for thee :
He in Christ that wealth is heaping,   40
Whom, whilst fighting, Christ is keeping
    For the palm of victory.

Nescit sancti nox obscurum,
Ut in pœnis quid impurum
 Fide tracta dubia ;   45
Neque cæcis lumen daret,
Si non eum radiaret
 Luminis præsentia.

Fidei confessio
Lucet in Laurentio :   50
Non ponit sub modio,
Statuit in medio
 Lumen coram omnibus.
Juvat Dei famulum
Crucis suæ bajulum,   55
Assum quasi ferculum,
Fieri spectaculum
 Angelis et gentibus.

Non abhorret prunis volvi,
Qui de carne cupit solvi   60
 Et cum Christo vivere ;
Neque timet occidentes
Corpus, sed non prævalentes
 Animam occidere.

Sicut vasa figulorum   65
Probat fornax, et eorum
 Solidat substantiam,

Darkness knows the saint's night never,
So that sin should mingle ever
　　With his pangs through faith too dim : 45
Nor the blind could he have lightened,
Had no light within him brightened
　　By its presence all for him.

Our true faith, confest aright,
Shines in Lawrence, pure and bright ;　50
'Neath no bushel placed, its light
In the midst, in all men's sight,
　　Sets he that it may be seen.
When to bear his cross thus bade,
As God's servant, he is glad,　　　55
That he, 'mid the fierce flames laid,
Should a spectacle be made
　　Both to angels and to men.

Flames he minds not, round him wrapping,
Who from flesh would be escaping,　　60
　　And abide with Christ for aye :
Neither fears he those men ever,
Who the body kill, but never,
　　Though they would, the soul can slay.

As the furnace tests by baking　　　65
Potters' vessels, harder making
　　The materials used thereby ;

Sic et ignis hunc assatum
Velut testam solidatum
 Reddit per constantiam.   70

Nam cum vetus corrumpatur,
Alter homo solidatur
 Veteris incendio ;
Unde nimis confortatus
Est athletæ principatus   75
 In Dei servitio.

  Hunc ardorem
   Factum foris
  Putat rorem
   Vis amoris   80
 Et zelus justitiæ ;
  Ignis urens,
  Non comburens,
  Vincit prunas
  Quas adunas,   85
 O minister impie.

  Parum sapis
  Vim sinapis,
  Si non tangis,
  Si non frangis ;   90
  Et plus fragrat
  Quando flagrat
Thus injectum ignibus.

So too this man, roast to cinders,
Hard as tiles the fire's heat renders
   Through untiring constancy.   70

For, as the old man decayeth
In the flame that round him playeth,
   Firmer yet becomes the new;
While that champion's power receiveth
Thus a rare support, who giveth   75
   Unto God the service due.

      Flames up-soaring,
        A dew-shower,
      Downward pouring,
        Through love's power,   80
   And zeal Godward, counteth he :
      Fire that warmeth,
      Yet nought harmeth,
      The live fuel
      Quenches, cruel   85
   Officer ! heaped up by thee !

      Scarce one learneth
      Mustard burneth,
      Till one use it,
      Till one bruise it;   90
      And then sweetest,
      When thou heatest
   It by fire, is incense too :

II.   M

Sic arctatus
Et assatus,   95
Sub ardore,
Sub labore,
Dat odorem
Pleniorem
Martyr de virtutibus.   100

O Laurenti ! laute nimis,
Rege victo rex sublimis,
Regis regum fortis miles,
Qui duxisti pœnas viles
    Certans pro justitia ;   105
Qui tot mala devicisti
Contemplando bona Christi,
Fac nos malis insultare,
Fac de bonis exsultare
    Meritorum gratia.   Amen.   110

So, limbs fastened,
By fire chastened, 95
'Neath its fury,
Sick and sorry,
Fuller flavour,
Sweeter savour,
Martyrs o'er their virtues throw. 100

Lawrence, beyond measure glorious!
King sublime, o'er kings victorious!
Who, in righteousness defending,
Countedst anguish cheap, contending
Bravely for the King of kings! 105
Who so many ills o'ercomest,
Looking to Christ's good things promised,
Make us tread down aught distressing,
Make us joy in every blessing,
Through the grace thy merit brings! Amen. 110

LXV.

ASSUMPTIO BEATÆ MARIÆ VIRGINIS.

xv° Augusti.

G RATULEMUR in hac die
　In qua Sanctæ fit Mariæ
　　Celebris Assumptio ;
Dies ista, dies grata,
Quâ de terris est translata   5
　In cœlum cum gaudio.

Super choros exaltata
Angelorum, est prælata
　Cunctis cœli civibus.
In decore contemplatur   10
Natum suum, et precatur
　Pro cunctis fidelibus.

Expurgemus nostras sordes
Ut illius, mundicordes,
　Assistamus laudibus ;   15

LXV.

THE ASSUMPTION OF THE BLESSED VIRGIN MARY.

AUGUST 15TH.

G LAD thanks let us Godward carry,
For the Assumption of St. Mary,
Which distinguishes this day :
'Tis a day with gladness mated,
When she was with joy translated   5
Up to heaven from earth away!

O'er angelic choirs uplifted,
She with higher rank was gifted
Than all heaven's own home-born sons.
In His beauty she surveyeth   10
There her Son, and there she prayeth
For all true and faithful ones.

Let us purge out sin's foul traces,
That we thus may in her praises
With hearts purified take part :   15

Si concordant linguis mentes,
Aures ejus intendentes
   Erunt nostris vocibus.

Nunc concordes hanc laudemus
Et in laude proclamemus :   20
   Ave, plena gratia !
Ave, virgo mater Christi,
Quæ de sancti concepisti
   Spiritus præsentia !

Virgo sancta, virgo munda,   25
Tibi nostræ sit jocunda
   Vocis modulatio.
Nobis opem fer desursum,
Et post hujus vitæ cursum
   Tuo junge filio.   30

Tu a sæclis præelecta,
Litterali diu tecta
   Fuisti sub cortice ;
De te, Christum genitura,
Prædixerunt in Scriptura   35
   Prophetæ, sed typice.

Sacramentum patefactum
Est, dum Verbum caro factum
   Ex te nasci voluit,

For her ears will listen ever
To our voices, if we never
   Discord make 'twixt tongue and heart.

With one heart now let us bless her,
And, while blessing, thus address her,   20
   " Hail, thou who such grace dost boast !
Hail to thee, Christ's mother-maiden !
With thy sacred burden laden
   By the o'ershading Holy Ghost !

" Holy Virgin ! spotless Virgin !   25
May our voices, upward surging,
   Pleasant music to thee bear :
Bring us help, from heaven descended,
And, when this life's course is ended,
   With thy Son unite us there !   30

" Thou, from all time pre-elected,
Wast for ages undetected
   'Neath the letter of God's law,
Where, that thou should'st Christ be bearing,
Prophets of thee, truth declaring,   35
   Spake in types in days of yore.

" Plain the mystery becometh,
When the Word our flesh assumeth,
   Of thee willing to be born,

Quod sua nos pietate   40
A maligni potestate
    Potentur eripuit.

Te per thronum Salomonis,
Te per vellus Gedeonis
    Præsignatam credimus   45
Et pur rubum incombustum,
Testamentum si vetustum,
    Mystice perpendimus.

Super vellus ros descendens
Et in rubo flamma splendens,   50
    (Neutrum tamen læditur,)
Fuit Christus carnem sumens,
In te tamen non consumens
    Pudorem, dum gignitur.

De te virga progressurum   55
Florem mundo profuturum
    Isaïas cecinit,
Flore Christum præfigurans
Cujus virtus semper durans
    Nec cœpit, nec desinit.   60

Fontis vitæ tu cisterna,
Ardens, lucens es lucerna ;
Per te nobis lux superna
    Suum fudit radium ;

Who hath, in His love most tender,   40
Been for us a strong defender,
    And our race from Satan torn.

" Type of thee we hold the gilded
Throne that Solomon erst builded,
    Type too Gideon's fleece, to be,   45
And the bush that never burneth :
If the mind aright discerneth
    The old Scriptures' mystery.

" O'er the fleece the dewdrops flowing,
In the bush the bright flame glowing,   50
    Though uninjured both remain,
Point to Christ, who flesh receiveth,
And who yet thy chasteness leaveth
    Unimpaired by travail-pain.

" From thee, as the rod, there springeth   55
Fairest flower, Isaiah singeth,
    Which shall all the world befriend ;
Christ in this fair flower forecasting ;
Him, whose virtue, ever lasting,
    Ne'er began and ne'er shall end.   60

" Cistern, whence life's fountain floweth !
Lamp, that with warm radiance gloweth !
'Tis through thee that heaven's light throweth
    Down on us its rays so bright !

Ardens igne caritatis,   65
Luce lucens castitatis,
Lucem summæ claritatis
    Mundo gignens Filium.

O salutis nostræ porta,
Nos exaudi, nos conforta,   70
Et a via nos distorta
    Revocare propera :
Te vocantes de profundo,
Navigantes in hoc mundo,
Nos ab hoste furibundo   75
    Tua prece libera !

Jesu, nostrum salutare,
Ob meritum singulare
Tuæ matris, visitare
In hac valle nos dignare   80
    Tuæ dono gratiæ ;
Qui neminem vis damnari.
Sic directe conversari
Nos concedas in hoc mari,
Ut post mortem munerari   85
    Digni simus requie !   Amen.

All the warmth of true love sharing,   65
Bright with Virgin light appearing,
To the world thine offspring bearing,
    The effulgence of God's Light !

" O thou gate of man's salvation !
Hear us, give us consolation,   70
And without least hesitation
    Call us back whene'er we stray :
From the deep we call thee, wailing ;
Whilst on this world's ocean sailing,
Save us through thy prayer availing   75
    From our furious foe, we pray !

" Jesu, who art our salvation !
For the due commemoration
Of Thy mother's worth and station,
With Thy grace's free dotation   80
    This our vale to visit deign :
Thou, who would'st that no man living
Perish, help to us be giving,
That, amid this ocean striving
To live well, at death arriving,   85
    We may fitly rest obtain ! "   Amen.

ASSUMPTIO BEATÆ MARIÆ VIRGINIS.

xv° Augusti.

A VE, Virgo singularis,
Mater nostri salutaris,
Quæ vocaris *Stella Maris*,
   Stella non erratica :
Nos in hujus vitæ mari   5
Non permitte naufragari,
Sed pro nobis salutari
   Tuo semper supplica

Sævit mare, fremunt venti,
Fluctus surgunt turbulenti,   10
Navis currit, sed currenti
   Tot occurrunt obvia;
Hic sirenes voluptatis,
Draco, canes, cum piratis,
Mortem pene desperatis   15
   Hæc intentant omnia.

LXVI.

THE ASSUMPTION OF THE BLESSED VIRGIN MARY.

AUGUST 15TH.

VIRGIN, hail! alone the fairest!
 Mother, who our Saviour barest!
And the name of *Sea-Star* wearest,
 Star that leadeth not astray!
On the sea of this life never   5
Let us suffer wreck, but ever
To thy Saviour, to deliver
 Those who travel o'er it, pray.

Seethes the sea, the storm-blast bloweth,
Wild the billows' tumult groweth,   10
Speeds our bark, but, as it goeth,
 By what crosses is it met!
Siren pleasures' wanton wooing,
Dragon, pirates, dogs, pursuing,
All these threaten death and ruin   15
 To men well-nigh desperate.

Post abyssos, nunc ad cœlum,
Furens unda fert phaselum ;
Nutat malus, fluit velum,
　　Nautæ cessat opera ;　　　　　　20
Contabescit in his malis
Homo noster animalis :
Tu nos, mater spiritalis,
　　Pereuntes libera.

Tu, perfusa cœli rore,　　　　　　25
Castitatis salvo flore,
Novum florem novo more
　　Protulisti sæculo.
Verbum Patri coæquale
Corpus intrans virginale　　　　　　30
Fit pro nobis corporale
　　Sub ventris umbraculo.

Te prævidit et elegit
Qui potenter cuncta regit,
Nec pudoris claustra fregit　　　　　　35
　　Sacra replens viscera ;
Nec pressuram, nec dolorem,
Contra primæ matris morem,
Pariendo Salvatorem
　　Sensisti, puerpera !　　　　　　40

Now deep down, now up to heaven,
Is our bark by fierce waves driven;
Nods the mast, its full sail riven,
   Till the seaman strives no more ;   20
Fast away, such evils tasting,
Is our human life-breath wasting :
Save us, to destruction hasting,
   Holy Mother ! we implore.

Sprinkled o'er with heaven's dew-shower,   25
Still intact thy chasteness' flower,
A new flower by new power
   Forth from thee on earth hath come.
Equal to the Sire in Godhead,
In thy Virgin frame secluded,   30
Was the Word for us embodied,
   Hidden in thy sheltering womb.

Thou by Him wast pre-elected,
By Whom all things are directed,
Who thy maiden-mark protected,   35
   When thy sacred womb He filled ;
Parent of our Saviour-brother !
Thou didst feel nor pain nor other
Sorrow, like to man's first mother,
   When thou broughtest forth that Child.   40

O Maria, pro tuorum
Dignitate meritorum,
Supra choros angelorum
    Sublimaris unice :
Felix dies hodierna   45
Qua conscendis ad superna !
Pietate tu materna
    Nos in imo respice.

Radix sancta, radix viva,
Flos, et vitis, et oliva,   50
Quam nulla vis insitiva
    Juvit ut fructificet,
Lampas soli, splendor poli,
Qui splendore præes soli,
Nos assigna tuæ proli,   55
    Ne districte judicet.

In conspectu summi Regis,
Sit pusilli memor gregis
Qui transgressor datæ legis
    Præsumit de venia :   60
Judex mitis et benignus,
Judex jugi laude dignus
Reis spei dedit pignus,
    Crucis factus hostia.

Mary ! for thy merits wholly
Hast thou been uplifted solely,
O'er the choirs of angels holy,
　　To a lofty throne above :
Joy is to this day pertaining,　　　　　　　45
When the heavens thou art gaining ;
Then on us, below remaining,
　　Look thou with maternal love !

Holy root, that never diest !
Flower, vine, olive, that suppliest　　　　50
Thine own power, and fructifiest
　　Without foreign graft or seed !
Sunbeams' light and heaven's bright glory !—
E'en the sun's self pales before thee !—
To Thy Son commend our story,　　　　55
　　And against strict justice plead.

There, before the King of heaven,
Think of this poor flock sore driven,
Which, transgressing God's law given,
　　Dares to look for clemency :　　　　60
For that Judge, Whom love so graces,
Judge deserving endless praises,
'Spite our guilt our hopes high raises,
　　Crucified upon the tree.

Jesu, sacri ventris fructus,   65
Nobis inter mundi fluctus
Sis via, dux, et conductus
    Liber ad cœlestia:
Tene clavum, rege navem,
Tu procellam sede gravem,   70
Portum nobis da suavem
    Pro tua clementia.   Amen.

Jesu, fruit of womb most holy !   65
'Mid the storms of this world's folly
Be our way, guide, leader, solely
    To the realms of heaven above !
Seize the helm, our vessel steer Thou,
Off the threatening tempest clear Thou,   70
And our vessel onward bear Thou
    To Thy pleasant port in love ! Amen.

S. BARTOLOMÆUS.

xxiv° Augusti.

L AUDEMUS omnes inclyta
 Bartolomæi merita :
Cujus sacra solemnia
Nobis inspirant gaudia.

Per diem centum vicibus   5
Flexis orabat genibus,
Nec minus noctis tempore,
Toto prostratus corpore.

In ipsius præsentia
Obmutescunt dæmonia ;   10
Christi sonante buccina,
Falsa terrentur numina.

Non Astaroth illudere
Genti permisit miseræ ;
Nec fallere, nec lædere,   15
Nec læsis potest parcere.

LXVII.

ST. BARTHOLOMEW.

AUGUST 24TH.

COME, let us all with praises now
Bartholomew's rare merits show,
Whose sacred feast-day here below
Makes all our hearts with gladness glow.

He used an hundred times a day   5
Upon his bended knees to pray ;
Nor through the hours of night did he,
Laid prostrate, pray less frequently.

Wherever he was present here
The very devils dumb appear ;   10
When he, Christ's trumpet, soundeth clear,
False gods and idols quake for fear.

He would not Ashtaroth allow
With lies an hapless race to cow :
Nor cheat, nor hurt, them can he now,   15
Nor pity for his victims show.

Gravi dignus supplicio
Cruciatur incendio;
Quanta fit ejus tortio
Berith patet indicio.   20

Per virtutes Apostoli
Patescit fraus diaboli.
Arte detecta subdoli,
Cultores cessant idoli.

Liber exultat Pseustius,   25
    Hostis repressa rabie,
Credit et rex Polymnius,
    Propter salutem filiæ.

Percussus ab Apostolo
Dæmon mugit ex idolo :   30
"A vobis ultra, miseri,
Sacra non posco fieri.

"Me jam nil posse fateor,
Qui vix respirans torqueor;
Ante diem judicii   35
Pœnam ferens incendii."

Sic effatus disparuit
Et sigilla comminuit;
Sed nec præsentes terruit,
Nam virtus crucis affuit.   40

He, worthy of grave punishment,
To writhe 'mid fires of hell is sent;
Where by what torments he is rent
From Berith's tale is evident.   20

Through this Apostle's might alone
The devil's fraud is fully shown;
And, when his cunning craft is known,
No followers more the idol own.

Pseustius exulted, when relieved   25
    From demon's rage, held 'neath control:
And king Polymnius believed,
    Because his daughter was made whole.

As 'neath the Apostle's stroke he lies,
The demon from the idol cries;   30
" From you, my wretched votaries!
I ask no further sacrifice.

" Powerless I am, I now declare,
Who scarce can breathe in torture here:
Before the judgment-day appear,   35
The punishment by fire I bear!"

He disappeared, as thus he spake,
And his own idol-image brake;
But made none present fear nor quake:
The Cross was there his place to take.   40

Christi signat charactere
  Fanum manus angelica:
Læsos absolvit libere
  Potestate mirifica.

Mox pellem mutat India,   45
Tincta baptismi gratia;
Ruga carens et macula,
Cœlesti gaudet copula.

Currunt ergo pontifices
Ad Astyagem supplices,   50
Athletam jam emeritum
Poscentes ad interitum.

Sub Christi testimonio,
Caput objecit gladio;
Sic triumphavit hodie   55
Doctor et victor Indiæ.

Bartolomæe, postula
Pro servis prece sedula,
Ut post vitæ curricula
Christum laudent in sæcula. Amen. 60

With Christ's own mark, the Cross's sign,
    An angel's fingers mark the fane,
And thence, through wondrous power divine,
    The vexed free absolution gain.

White through baptismal grace we see   45
India, so dark-hued formerly ;
Without a spot, from wrinkle free,
Thus joined to heaven it joys to be.

Their high-priests to Astyages
Then hasten, and, upon their knees,   50
Demand that he at once will slay
The champion, victor in the fray.

To witness thus for Christ his Lord,
His head he bowed beneath the sword ;
So he this day, as victor, shone,   55
Who India taught and India won.

In constant prayer God's throne before,
For us, Bartholomew ! implore,
That we, when this life's course is o'er,
May sing Christ's praise for evermore ! Amen. 60

S. AUGUSTINUS.

XXVIII° AUGUSTI.

ÆTERNI festi gaudia
　　Nostra sonet harmonia,
Quo mens in se pacifica
Vera frequentat sabbata ;

Mundi cordis lætitia　　　　　5
Odorans vera gaudia,
Quibus prægustat avida
Quæ sit sanctorum gloria,

Qua lætatur in patria
Cœlicolarum curia,　　　　　10
Regem donantem præmia
Sua cernens in gloria.

Beata illa patria
Quæ nescit nisi gaudia !
Nam cives hujus patriæ　　　　15
Non cessant laudes canere.

LXVIII.

ST. AUGUSTINE.

AUGUST 28TH.

OUR tuneful strains let us upraise
  That endless feast's delights to praise,
When, since thereon no trouble weighs,
The heart observes true sabbath days;

The rapture of a conscience clear,   5
That perfumes all those joys sincere,
By which it hath rich foretaste here
Of saints' unending glory *there*,

Where the celestial company
Joys in its home exultingly;   10
And, giving crowns, their King they see
In all his glorious majesty.

O happy land! how great its bliss,
That knoweth nought but happiness!
For all the dwellers on that shore   15
One ceaseless song of praise outpour;

Quos ille dulcor afficit
Quem nullus mœror inficit;
Quos nullus hostit impetit
Nullusque turbo concutit ;   20

Ubi dies clarissima
Melior est quam millia,
Luce lucens præfulgida,
Plena Dei notitia;

Quam mens humana capere,   25
Nec lingua valet promere,
Donec vitæ victoria
Commutet hæc mortalia.

Quando Deus est omnia :
Vita, virtus, scientia,   30
Victus, vestis et cætera,
Quæ velle potest mens pia !

Hoc in hac valle misera
Meditetur mens sobria;
Hoc per soporem sentiat,   35
Hoc attendat dum vigilat ;

Quo mundi post exilia
Coronetur iu patria,
Ac in decoris gloria
Regem laudet per sæcula.   40

Who those delights' full sweetness feel,
Which not a trace of grief conceal ;
'Gainst whom no foeman draws the steel,
And who beneath no tempest reel :   20

Where one day, clear from cloudlet's haze,
Is better than a thousand days ;
Bright with true light's transcendent rays ;
Filled with that knowledge of God's ways,

To grasp which human reason fails,   25
Nor human tongue to tell avails,
Till this mortality shall be
Absorbed in that life's victory ;

When God shall all in all appear,
Life, righteousness, and knowledge clear ;   30
Victuals and vesture and whate'er
The pious mind would wish to share !

This in this vale of misery
The sober mind's chief thought should be ;
This should it feel, while rest it takes,   35
This should be with it when it wakes ;

How it will in that home,—its days
Of earthly exile past,—fond lays
For ever, crowned, the King to praise
In all His glorious beauty, raise.   40

Harum laudum præconia
Imitatur Ecclesia,
Dum recensentur annua
Sanctorum natalitia ;

Cum post peracta prælia   45
Digna redduntur præmia
Pro passione rosea,
Pro castitate candida.

Datur et torques aurea
Pro doctrina catholica :   50
Qua præfulget Augustinus
In summi regis curia.

Cujus librorum copia
Fides firmatur unica ;
Hinc et mater Ecclesia   55
Vitat errorum devia.

Hujus sequi vestigia
Ac prædicare dogmata
Fide recta ac fervida,
Det nobis mater gratia ! Amen.   60

These praises, sounding loud and clear,
The Church now imitateth here ;
As, in due order, year by year,
The birthdays of her saints appear ;

When, after they have fought their fight,   45
With worth-won honours they are dight ;
The martyr crowned with roses bright ;
The virgin clad in robes of white.

They too receive a golden chain,
Who doctrines Catholic maintain :   50
In which Augustine now doth reign,
One of the great King's shining train ;

Whose written volumes' full array
Are now the one Faith's strength and stay :
Hence Mother Church avoids the way   55
Where errors lead mankind astray.

To follow where his steps precede,
And preach the truths He taught indeed,
Mother ! may grace thy servants lead,
And grant the pure warm faith we need ! Amen. 60

S. AUGUSTINUS.

xxviii° Augusti.

D E profundis tenebrarum
   Mundo lumen exit clarum
Et scintillat hodie :
Olim quidem vas erroris,
Augustinus vas honoris   5
   Datus est Ecclesiæ.

Verbo Dei dum obedit,
Credit errans et accedit
   Ad baptismi gratiam ;
Quam in primis tuebatur,   10
Verbis, scriptis exsecratur
   Erroris fallaciam.

Firmans fidem, formans mores,
Legis sacræ perversores
   Verbi necat gladio ;   15
Obmutescit Fortunatus ;
Cedunt Manes et Donatus
   Tantæ lucis radio.

LXIX.

ST. AUGUSTINE.

AUGUST 28TH.

FROM the depths of dark obscurest
  Comes forth light, which shines, the purest,
On the earth to-day from heaven :
Once a vessel, truth mistrusting,
Now for honour made, Augustine   5
  To the Church of God was given.

He, the Word of God obeying,
Now believes, once from it straying,
  And for grace to baptism comes :
He those errors, once commended,   10
And in youth with words defended,
  Reprobates in written tomes.

Faith confirming, precepts framing,
Those, against Christ's law declaiming,
  Slays he with the Word's sharp sword :   15
Fortunatus' utterance faileth,
Manes with Donatus quaileth,
  'Neath such radiant light outpoured.

II.   O

Mundus marcens et inanis,
Et doctrinis doctus vanis　　　20
　　Per pestem hæreticam,
Multum cœpit fructum ferre,
Dum in fines orbis terræ
　　Fidem sparsit unicam.

Clericalis vitæ formam　　　25
Conquadravit juxta normam
　　Coetus apostolici :
Sui quippe nil habebant ;
Tanquam suum dividebant
　　In commune clerici.　　　30

Sic multorum pro salute
Diu vivens in virtute
Bona tandem senectute
　　Dormivit cum patribus.
In extremis nil legavit　　　35
Qui suum nil æstimavit,
Immo totum reputavit
　　Commune cum fratribus.

Salve, gemma confessorum,
Lingua Christi, vox cœlorum,　　　40
Tuba vitæ, lux doctorum,
　　Præsul beatissime ;

Earth, made void and fast expiring,
But vain doctrines' lore acquiring,   20
   Through the pest of heresy,
To produce much fruit commences,
As the one Faith he dispenses
   To its furthest boundary.

Rules he made for priestly living;   25
As their pattern, to them giving
   The Apostles' company :
Nought their own these priests computed,
But whate'er seemed theirs devoted
   To the whole community.   30

Thus, for many's welfare striving,
Many years in virtue living,
At a good old age arriving,
   With his sires he slept at last.
No bequests he left, when dying,   35
Who, its ownership denying,
Thought his wealth should be supplying
   All with whom his lot was cast.

Hail, Confessors' gem bright burning !
Tongue of Christ ! heaven's voice of warning ! 40
Trump of life and light of learning !
   Prelate high amongst the blest !

Qui te patrem venerantur,
Te doctorem, consequantur
Vitam in qua gloriantur   45
    Beatorum animæ.   Amen.

May those, Father! who revere thee,
'Neath thy guidance that life near thee
Gain, where joys the truest cheer thee   45
   In the Saints' all-glorious rest!   Amen.

DECOLLATIO DIVINI JOHANNIS BAPTISTÆ.

XXIX° AUGUSTI.

PRÆCURSOREM summi regis
Et præconem novæ legis
Celebrat Ecclesia.
In hac luce tam festiva,
Gaude, mater, et votiva   5
Deprome præconia.

Hujus ortum veneremur,
Sed nec minus delectemur
In ejus martyrio.
Totus mundus sit jocundus!   10
Nulli martyr hic secundus
Virtute vel præmio.

Non est nostræ pravitatis
Virum tantæ sanctitatis
Laudare per omnia.   15
Summa rei recitetur,
Ut affectus inflammetur
Ex ejus memoria.

LXX.

THE BEHEADING OF ST. JOHN
BAPTIST.

AUGUST 29TH.

J OHN, the King of kings' precursor,
  John, the new Law's bold rehearser,
    Celebrates the Church to-day !
Mother ! on so glad a morning
Joy, with praise his name adorning,   5
    And bring forth a votive lay !

Let us keep his birthday rightly,
But rejoice we no less brightly
    In the martyrdom he won.
Show, Creation ! exultation ;   10
Second is this martyr's station,
    In both mark and meed, to none !

'Tis not for our fallen nature
To extol each single feature
    Of such special sanctity :   15
Be the tale in sum repeated ;
That our love may kindle, heated
    With his blessed memory.

Non arundo levitatis,
Sed columna veritatis   20
   Nulla palpat crimina ;
Scribas tangit et doctores,
Vocans legis transgressores
   Viperæ genimina.

Arguebat hic Herodem,   25
Nec terretur ab eodem
   Ligatus in carcere.
Fert injuste justus pœnam,
Rem detestans tam obscœnam
   Regis et adulteræ.   30

Sævit in hunc vis tyranni :
Laus accrescit hinc Johanni,
   Tyranno supplicium ;
Stultus servit sapienti,
Quia justus in præsenti   35
   Purgatur per impium.

In natalis sui cœna
Capitali plecti pœna
   Johannem rex imperat.
Spiculator saltatrici,   40
Saltatrix dat genetrici
   Caput quod petierat.

He, no reed to bend and quiver,
But Truth's pillar, firm for ever,   20
   Never calleth evil good ;
Scribes he strikes at and professors,
Calling all the Law's transgressors
   Offspring of a viper's brood.

Herod's sin he censured gravely ;   25
Bound by him, he bore up bravely,
   In a prison kept secure :
Pains unjust the just endureth,
Who such filthiness abhorreth
   In the king and paramour.   30

Tyrant power against him burneth :
Whence John greater honour earneth,
   And the tyrant torments dure :
Help to wisdom folly giveth,
Since the just, while here he liveth,   35
   By the impious is made pure.

At his birthday-feast at even
Orders by the king are given,
   That the head of John be brought.
She who danced that head receiveth   40
From the officer, and giveth
   To her mother what she sought.

Crux præsignat sublimari
Christum, sed hunc minorari
 Capitis abscissio.   45
Mors est justi pretiosa
Quam præcessit gloriosa
 Vitæ conversatio.

Nos ad laudem tui, Christe,
Præcursoris et Baptistæ   50
 Colimus solemnia.
Tu nos ab hac mortis valle,
Duc ad vitam recto calle
 Per ejus vestigia.   Amen.

Christ's increase the Cross foreshoweth,
But, that less the Baptist groweth,
   His beheading shadows forth.   45
Precious, if the life preceding
Glory o'er that life were shedding,
   Is the righteous' death on earth.

Christ ! the better to adore Thee
Through the Baptist sent before Thee,   50
   We this feast-day celebrate :
Out of death's dark valley lead us
Thither, where his steps precede us,
   And our path to life make straight ! Amen.

LXXI.

S. ÆGIDIUS.

1° SEPTEMBRIS.

CONGAUDENTES exultemus,
    Exultantes celebremus
        Ægidii solemnia,
Qui triumphans de terrenis
Coronandus in supernis   5
        Summa petit gaudia!

Hunc insignem pietate,
Virum plenum sanctitate,
        Stirpe natum regia,
Templum Deo mox futurum,   10
Mundo satis profuturum
        Procreavit gratia.

Qui in primo ævi flore
Quantus floret in virore
        Præmonstravit gratia ;   15
Data veste mendicanti
Confert diu languescenti
        Salutis remedia.

LXXI.

ST. GILES.

SEPTEMBER 1ST.

L ET us joy with exultation,
 And, exulting, celebration
  Make to-day of Giles's rites,
Who, o'er things of earth victorious,
Seeks those joys of all most glorious,   5
  And a crown in heavenly heights !

He, for piety most noted,
Full of holiness devoted,
  Scion of a regal race,
Soon to be God's holy temple,   10
And earth's very bright example,
  Was begotten of God's grace.

In his youth's first early flower,
What in riper age his power
  Would be, he, through grace, foreshowed ; 15
Clothing to a beggar giving,
Medicine too, his health reviving,
  He on him, long sick, bestowed.

Hinc, post mortem genitorum,
Plenus laude meritorum,   20
   Sua vendens omnia,
Larga manu dat egenis,
Egens ipse, alienis,
   Exsulat a patria.

Undis nautæ fatigati   25
Portum petunt liberati
   Per ejus suffragia;
Medicina dum rogatur,
Sanitati revocatur
   Vidualis filia.   30

Pellitur sterilitas,
Succedit fertilitas,
   Surgit messis copia.
Ægri reparatio,
Pulso morbi vitio,   35
   Mœstis fit lætitia.

Ad deserta sitiens
Properavit, fugiens
   Hominum consortia.
Panis ubi deerat,   40
Christus tamen aderat
   Parando cibaria;

When his parents died, o'erflowing
With the praise due to well-doing,   20
 Selling all, with open hand
Needy strangers he endoweth,
And, himself a pauper, goeth,
 Exiled, from his native land.

Sailors, tempest-tost and wearied,   25
To the port they seek are carried,
 Rescued by his earnest prayer :
To a widow he restoreth
Whole her child, while she imploreth
 A physician in despair.   30

 Barrenness away is chased,
 By fertility replaced,
  And a plenteous harvest comes :
Sick men with new health are filled,
Dire diseases thence expelled,   35
 Causing joy in mournful homes.

 To a bare and barren waste,
 Sore athirst, he then made haste,
  To escape from man's abode.
Christ Himself was present there,—   40
Since but scanty was the fare,—
 To provide His servant's food ;

Fame ne deficeret,
Affuit, quæ pasceret
   Virum Dei, bestia.   45

Sic latere voluit;
Sed latentem reperit
   Regalis familia.
Per nutricem cognitus,
A rege commonitus   50
   Struit monasteria.
Illic castra militum
Pro Christo certantium
   Collocavit fortia.

Hunc devote qui precatur   55
Voto regis non frustratur,
   Protestante Gallia;
Dum pro rege supplicatur
Qui commisso premebatur,
   Impetratur venia.   60

Mox nacturus præmia
Pro mundi victoria,
   Subiit cœlestia :
Quem cœli militia
Duxit ad palatia   65
   Ubi pax et gloria.

Lest of hunger he should die,
A wild animal drew nigh
  To sustain the man of God. 45

Hidden thus he fain would be,
But the royal family
  Of his place of hiding hear :
Through his nurse discovered, there
At the monarch's earnest prayer 50
  He a monastery near,—
Where he many a warrior bold,
In the cause of Christ enrolled,
  By his side encamped,—doth rear.

Through this monarch's prayer, whoever 55
Prays to Giles devoutly never,—
  France is witness,—prays in vain ;
For, when for the king he prayeth
On whose mind a dark deed weigheth,
  He his pardon doth obtain. 60

To receive those laurels soon
By his earthly triumphs won,
  Hath this saint to heaven gone,
Whom the host about God's throne
To those mansions, where alone 65
  Peace and glory are, led on.

Hujus festum veneremus,
Venerantes habeamus
    Semper in memoria.
Hunc submisse flagitemus,   70
Flagitantes imploremus
    Nobis dari gaudia,
Quo felices maneamus
Et cum sanctis decantemus
    Festivum alleluia!   Amen.   75

Giles's feast then venerate we,
Venerating, consecrate we
 In perpetual memory!
Humbly now let us entreat him,   70
And, entreating, supplicate him,
 That true joys our portion be,
Where in bliss that endeth never
We may Alleluias ever
 With the Saints sing joyfully! Amen. 75

S. ÆGIDIUS.

1° SEPTEMBRIS.

P ROMAT pia vox cantoris
   Hujus laudem confessoris !
Ipsum laudans, præsens chorus
Sit festivus et canorus !

Fide fuit Deo carus,   5
Mundo quoque stirpe clarus :
Mundi tamen sprevit fastum
Se conservans Deo castum.

Adhuc ævo puerili,
Sensu fuit tam subtili   10
Quod in brevi fit doctorum
Doctor ipse doctiorum.

Ardens intus caritate,
Foris lucet honestate ;
Intus ardens vis amoris   15
Per exemplum lucet foris.

LXXII.

ST. GILES.

SEPTEMBER 1ST.

L OVING hymns, Precentor ! bringing,
This Confessor's praise be singing !
To extol him, Choir ! before us
Sing this sweet and festive chorus !

Dear to God through faith devoted,   5
Of a race in this world noted,
Earthly pomps he scorned still, striving
Pure in God's sight to be living.

In his years of boyhood even
Such great parts to him were given,   10
That the teacher soon he turnèd
E'en of teachers the most learnèd.

He, within, with warm love gloweth,
And, without, bright virtues showeth;
Love's strong heat, within residing,   15
Shines without, all others guiding.

Dum languenti præbet vestem
Mox languoris fugat pestem,
Ex divina dans virtute
Vestem simul cum salute.   20

Quidquid rerum possidebat
Christo dedit quem colebat ;
Fit egenus, ut egeni
Fiant bonis ejus pleni.

Dum egenis hoc impendit   25
Christus ei plus rependit ;
Dans pro Christo transitura
Promeretur permansura.

Quod fateri rex veretur
Scelus scire promeretur ;   30
Christus ei revelavit
Scelus quod rex perpetravit.

Nam altari dum astaret
Dumque missam celebraret,
De supernis charta missa   35
Regis pandit huic commissa.

Hic horrendæ rei reum
Videns crimen apud Deum,
Jam pro rege supplex orat
Cujus culpam non ignorat.   40

To one sick his robe he sendeth,
And his sickness straightway endeth ;
Thus at once, through power from heaven,
Clothes and health by him are given.   20

All his riches he surrendered,
And to Christ, as offerings, tendered :
Needy he became to feed them
With his goods, who most did need them.

Whilst he on the poor thus spendeth,   25
Greater wealth to him Christ sendeth ;
Off for Christ things temporal casting,
He obtains those everlasting.

Of the crime a monarch feareth
To confess to him he heareth ;   30
Christ to him the facts revealing
Of the monarch's evil dealing.

For whilst, at the altar waiting,
He a mass was celebrating,
From above a scroll descended,   35
Telling how the king offended.

Having thus dread insight given
To a deed abhorred of heaven,
Now in humble prayer he boweth
For the king whose crime he knoweth.   40

Servo Dei non ingratum
Præbet cerva famulatum :
Servit cerva nutu Dei,
Quasi grates agens ei.

Plura possunt reperiri   45
Mira facta sancti viri,
Quibus clare demonstratur
Quam præclarus habeatur.

Hic præsentem juvet chorum
Ut in regno beatorum   50
Regem videns sempiternum
Glorietur in æternum.   Amen.

Help he from a hind receiveth,
Which in gratitude she giveth ;
Moved by God, her succour tendering,
As it were thanks to him rendering.

Far more deeds with marvel glowing   45
Might be found of this Saint's doing,
Showing us to demonstration
How illustrious is his station.

To this choir his help be given,
That they evermore in heaven,   50
Gazing on the King eternal,
Glory with the Saints supernal !   Amen.

LXXIII.

NATIVITAS BEATÆ MARIÆ VIRGINIS.

VIII° Septembris.

SALVE, mater Salvatoris,
Vas electum, vas honoris.
   Vas cœlestis gratiæ ;
Ab æterno vas provisum,
Vas insigne, vas excisum   5
   Manu Sapientiæ !

Salve, Verbi sacra parens,
Flos de spinis, spina carens,
   Flos, spineti gloria !
Nos spinetum, nos peccati   10
Spina sumus cruentati,
   Sed tu spinæ nescia.

Porta clausa, fons hortorum,
Cella custos unguentorum,
   Cella pigmentaria :   15

LXXIII.

THE NATIVITY OF THE BLESSED VIRGIN MARY.

September 8th.

H AIL to thee, our Saviour's mother !
Vessel, honoured o'er all other !
Chosen vessel of God's grace !
Vessel, known before creation !
Noble vessel, whose formation   5
'Neath the All-wise hand took place !

Hail, the world's own mother holy !
Sprung from thorns, but thornless throughly !
Flower a thornbrake's glory born !
We the thornbrake are, surrounded   10
With sin's thorns, and by them wounded,
But thou art without a thorn.

Closed gate ! fount through gardens pouring !
Storehouse, precious spikenard storing!
Store of unguents sweet to smell !   15

Cinnamomi calamum,
Myrrham, thus et balsamum
   Superas fragrantia.

Salve, decus virginum,
Mediatrix hominum,   20
   Salutis puerpera ;
Myrtus temperantiæ,
Rosa patientiæ,
   Nardus odorifera !

Tu convallis humilis,   25
Terra non arabilis,
   Quæ Deum parturiit ;
Flos campi, convallium
Singulare lilium,
   Christus ex te prodiit.   30

Tu cœlestis paradisus
Libanusque non incisus,
   Vaporans dulcedinem :
Tu candoris et decoris,
Tu dulcoris et odoris   35
   Habes plenitudinem.

Tu thronus es Salomonis,
Cui nullus par in thronis
   Arte vel materia :

Cinnamon's sweet-scented reed,
Incense, balsam, myrrh, indeed
    Thou in fragrance dost excel !

Hail, fair type of maiden grace ;
Mediatrix of man's race !   20
    Of salvation brought to bed !
Continence's myrtle-tree !
Rose of love and clemency !
    Nard whence sweetest scents are shed !

Lowliest of valleys thou,   25
Soil that never felt the plough,
    Which to God himself gave birth !
Meadow-flower ! lily fair !
Which the valley, peerless, bare !
    Christ of thee was born on earth !   30

O thou paradise in heaven !
Lebanon no axe hath riven,
    Breathing sweetness all around !
Virgin whiteness, beauty's brightness,
Finest flavours, sweetest savours,   35
    Plenteously in thee abound !

Thou the wise king's throne appearest,
Which, in shape and substance, fairest,
    'Mongst all thrones hath ever been :

Ebur candens castitatis,   40
Aurum fulvum charitatis
    Præsignant mysteria.

Palmam præfers singularem
Nec in terris habes parem,
    Nec in cœli curia ;   45
Laus humani generis,
Virtutum præ cæteris
    Tenes privilegia.

Sol luna lucidior,
    Et luna sideribus ;   50
Sic Maria dignior
    Creaturis omnibus.

Lux eclipsim nesciens
    Virginis est castitas,
Ardor indeficiens,   55
    Immortalis charitas.

(*Dum venerabilis Adam sequenti versiculo Beatam
Mariam Virginem salutaret, ab ea resalutari et re-
gratiari meruit.*)

SALVE, MATER PIETATIS,
ET TOTIUS TRINITATIS
    NOBILE TRICLINIUM.

Chastity in ivory's whiteness,   40
Charity in red gold's brightness,
  Shadowed forth, therein are seen.

Peerless is the palm thou bearest,
Peerless thou on earth appearest,
  And in heaven amongst the blest :   45
  As the praise of all man's race,
  Thee peculiar virtues grace,
    Given to thee above the rest.

As the sun outshines the moon,
  And the moon each twinkling star, 50
Mary is than every one
  Of God's creatures worthier far !

Light, that no eclipse can know,
  Is her virgin chastity ;
Heat, which ne'er will cease to glow,   55
  Her love's deathless constancy !

(*As the venerable Adam was saluting the Blessed
Virgin Mary in the following stanza, he was himself
in return saluted and thanked by her.*)

MOTHER OF FAIR LOVE, WE NAME THEE !
FAMED TRICLINIUM WE PROCLAIM THEE,
  WHICH THE TRINITY ALL SHARE ;

Verbi tamen incarnati   60
Speciale majestati
   Præparans hospitium !

O Maria, stella maris,
Dignitate singularis,
Super omnes ordinaris   65
   Ordines cœlestium :
In supremo sita poli,
Nos assigna tuæ Proli,
Ne terrores sive doli
   Nos supplantent hostium.   70

In procinctu constituti,
Te tuente simus tuti,
Pervicacis et versuti
Tuæ cedat vis virtuti,
   Dolus providentiæ.   75
Jesu, Verbum summi Patris,
Serva servos Tuæ matris,
Solve reos, salva gratis,
Et nos Tuæ claritatis
   Configura gloriæ.   Amen.   80

Though thou dost a special dwelling   60
For the majesty excelling
    Of the Incarnate Word prepare !

Mary, Star o'er ocean glowing !
Rival none in honour knowing !
Foremost in precedence going   65
    'Mongst all ranks around God's throne !
Placed in highest heaven, commend us
To thine Offspring to befriend us,
And from fear of foes defend us,
    Lest by guile we be o'erthrown.   70

Safe, in battle-line extended,
May we be, by thee defended ;
May foes' force and shrewdness blended
Bow before thy virtues splendid,
    And their craft 'neath thy foresight.   75
Christ the Word, God's generation !
Guard Thy mother's congregation ;
Pardon guilt, grant free salvation,
And with the illumination
    Of Thy glory make us bright ! Amen. 80

LXXIV.

NATIVITAS BEATÆ MARIÆ VIRGINIS.

VIII° SEPTEMBRIS.

L UX advenit veneranda,
Lux in choris jubilanda
Luminosis cordibus!
Hujus læta lux dieï
Festum refert matris Dei   5
Dedicandum laudibus.

Vox exultet
Modulata,
Mens resultet
Medullata,   10
Ne sit laus inutilis!
Sic laus Deo
Decantetur
Ut in eo
Collaudetur   15
Mater ejus nobilis!

Gloriosa
Dignitate,

LXXIV.

THE NATIVITY OF THE BLESSED
VIRGIN MARY.

September 8th.

D AWNS a day for adoration,
Day, when in glad jubilation
Songs enlightened hearts should raise !
This day's joyous light another
Feast-day brings round of God's mother, 5
Dedicated to her praise !

Voice ! now keep thou
Joyful measure ;
Heart ! now leap thou,
Filled with pleasure, 10
That your praise effective be !
Let God's glory
So be lauded,
That the story
Be applauded 15
Of his mother's dignity !

Great in splendour
Of her station ;

Viscerosa
 Pietate,   20
Compunctiva nomine,
 Cum honore
 Matronali,
 Cum pudore
  Virginali,   25
 Nitet cœli cardine.

Rubus quondam exardebat
Et tunc ardor non urebat
 Nec virori nocuit :
Sic ardore spiritali   30
Nec attactu conjugali
 Virgo Deum genuit.

Hæc est ille fons signatus,
Hortus clausus, fecundatus
 Virtutum seminibus.   35
Hæc est illa porta clausa,
Quam latente Deus causa
 Clauserat hominibus.

Hæc est vellus trahens rorem,
Plenus ager dans odorem, 40
 Cunctis terræ finibus.
Hæc est virga ferens florem,
Terra suum Salvatorem
 Germinans fidelibus.

Very tender
    In compassion,   20
Sorrowful is she by name ;
Honour-laden,
    As child-bearing ;
Still a maiden
    Pure appearing,   25
Bright in heaven's height shines her fame !

As of old the bush to Moses
Seems in flames, yet never loses
    Aught, by burning, of its green ;
So by spiritual graces,   30
Not by conjugal embraces,
    Hath a maid God's mother been.

She is that sealed fount, ne'er drying,
That walled garden, fructifying
    By the good seed in it sown :   35
She is that close-fastened portal,
Shut by God 'gainst every mortal
    For some secret cause unknown.

She that fleece is, which inviteth
Dew ; that rich field that delighteth   40
    With sweet scents all ends of earth :
She that rod is, blossoms bearing,
Soil for all, true faith declaring,
    To a Saviour giving birth.

Hæc est dicta per exemplum   45
Mons, castellum, aula, templum,
Thalamus et civitas :
Sic eidem aliorum
Assignatur electorum
Nominum sublimitas.   50

Cujus preces vitia,
Cujus nomen tristia,
Cujus odor lilia,
Cujus vincunt labia
    Favum in dulcedine.   55
Super vinum sapida,
Super nivem candida,
Super rosam rosida,
Super lunam lucida
    Veri Solis lumine.   60

    Imperatrix
      Supernorum,
    Superatrix
      Infernorum,
    Eligenda   65
      Via cœli,
    Retinenda
      Spe fideli,

She is titled, for example,   45
"Mountain," "Castle," "Hall," and "Temple,"
"Bridal Chamber," "Citadel":
To her now hath there been given,
Of sublimest names in heaven,
    That which doth the rest excel.   50

Whose petitions vices quell,
Whose name sorrow doth dispel,
Whose rare scents like lilies smell,
Whose sweet lips by far excel
    Honey's nectar in delight.   55
Daintier than the wine-cup's flow,
Whiter than the driven snow,
Fresher than rose, washed but now,
Brighter with the true Sun's glow
    Than the pale moon's orb by night.   60

    Queen o'er glorious
      Realms supernal,
    And victorious
      O'er infernal!
    All-availing   65
      Path to heaven,
    Whence unfailing
      Faith's ne'er driven!

Separatos
  A te longe,   70
Revocatos
  A te, junge
Tuorum collegio :
  Mater bona
    Quam rogamus,   75
  Nobis dona
    Quod optamus,
  Nec sic spernas
    Peccatores
Ut non cernas   80
    Precatores ;
Reos sibi
  Diffidentes,
Tuos tibi
  Confidentes   85
Tuo siste Filio ! Amen.

All those falling
From thee wholly,   70
Now recalling
From their folly,
With thine own once more unite !
O good Mother,
Whom we pray to !   75
Grant our other
Prayers to-day too ;
Sinners, straying,
Ne'er so spurn thou,
As from praying   80
Hearts to turn now :
Sinners, wholly
Self-diffiding,
With those, truly
Thine abiding,   85
Lead into thy dear Son's sight !   Amen.

LXXV.

NATIVITAS BEATÆ MARIÆ VIRGINIS.

VIII° SEPTEMBRIS.

A VE, mater Jesu Christi,
   Quæ de cœlo concepisti
    Non carnis commercio!
A contactu viri pura
Concepisti, paritura   5
    Gaudium cum gaudio.

Peperisti medicinam,
Non humanam, sed divinam
    Pereunti sæculo.
Totus mundus in languore,   10
Totus erat in dolore,
    Totus in periculo.

Mundi languor error ejus,
Quo languore nihil pejus,
    Nihil tam pestiferum;   15

LXXV.

THE NATIVITY OF THE BLESSED
VIRGIN MARY.

SEPTEMBER 8TH.

H AIL, O mother of Christ Jesus!
Who from heaven that Son so precious
Didst conceive uncarnally!
Pure from contact with aught human,
Thou conceivedst, who, as woman,   5
Should'st with joy Joy's parent be!

Thou hast borne a medicine, given
Not of man, but sprung from heaven,
To an age in swift decay:
All the world in great prostration,   10
All the world in tribulation,
All the world in peril, lay.

This world's sin was this world's weakness,
And there is no direr sickness,
None so deadly at the last;   15

Hostis totum possidebat,
Quia totus diffluebat
    Per abrupta scelerum.

Nondum semen venerat
Quod nobis promiserat   20
    Deus ab initio,
Semen ex muliere,
Sine carnis opere,
    Sine matris vitio.

Mulier eligitur,   25
Cujus serpens nititur
    Pungere calcaneum:
Sed fortis et sapiens,
Hosti non consentiens,
    Præcavet aculeum.   30

Caput anguis hæc contrivit,
Cujus carni counivit
    Se majestas Filii;
Sexus autem fragilis,
Sexus seductibilis   35
    Vires frangit impii.

Ave, virgo gloriosa,
Plus obryzo pretiosa,
    Fragrans super lilia !

Satan was in full possession,
Since down steeps of foul transgression
   All the world was gliding fast.

Not yet had that seed appeared,
Which God's promise had declared   20
   From the first to us should come;
Seed with woman as its source,
Without carnal intercourse,
   Sprung from mother's spotless womb.

Of a woman choice was made,   25
Whom that serpent old essayed
   In the heel to wound and tear :
But she, wise, and valiant too,
Made no compact with the foe,
   Of his deadly sting aware.   30

She, with whose flesh to be blended
God's Son's glory condescended,
   Bruised the subtle serpent's head :
Woman, though but weak and frail,
Doth to crush hell's power avail,   35
   Woman, easily misled !

Virgin, who in glory shinest !
Precious beyond gold the finest !
   Sweeter far than lilies ! hail !

Tibi cedit laus herbarum,   40
Florum decor et gemmarum,
   Libanique gloria !

O Maria, maris stella,
Pro conservis interpella
   Jugi prece Filium.   45
Quia jugis est assultus,
Jugis noster est singultus
   Et juge suspirium.

Te preces, te suspiria,
   Te nostri tangant gemitus ;   50
Te virtutis potentia
   Nequam refrena spiritus.

Ne carnis nos lubricitas
   Resolvat in flagitia,
Ne mundi juvet vanitas
   Christi juvante gratia !   Amen.

Meadows' fairness yields before thee; 40
Flowers', gems', beauty, with the glory
   Of proud Lebanon's forests, pale!

To thy Son, thou Star of Ocean!
Mary! ever with devotion
   For thy fellow-servants pray; 45
Since temptations are unending,
Endless are our sobs heart-rending,
   And our sighs from day to day.

O may our prayers, our sighs, our tears,
   With pity touch thine heart within; 50
And, by the power thy virtue bears,
   Do thou restrain what prompts to sin.

Let carnal ways, so smooth and bright,
   The means to misdeeds ne'er be made:
Nor this world's empty joys delight, 55
   With Christ's free grace at hand to aid! Amen.

NOTES.

II.   R

`

NOTES.

St. Vincent was a Spanish saint, martyred under the proconsul Dacian in the 4th century. The recital of his pious serenity and cheerfulness under unheard-of tortures, as detailed in this, and the two next, Sequences, is very striking. He seems to have been of noble family, and to have been ordained deacon by Valerius, the Bishop of Sarragossa, who, having an impediment in his speech, appears to have left the work of preaching the Gospel almost entirely to his more youthful companion, both in the ministry and in martyrdom.

Sequence XLI.

Vide note on the last Sequence.

13-18. Cf. Exod. v. 4, 5; xxvii. 9; xxvii. 16. *Purple* marks the martyr, *linen* the confessor; both of which St. Vincent was.

21-23. Cf. Exod. xxvi. 14.

24-26. Cf. Psalm cxxvi. 5, 6.

49. "Quod nunc est onus, erit honor." *August.* Serm. 277, 4.

SEQUENCE XLII.

Vide notes on the two preceding Sequences.
25-30. I have followed the text, as given by *Mone*, " Hymni
Latini," vol. iii. 558. Gautier's text is untranslatable.

SEQUENCE XLIII.

1-25. Cf. Acts ix.

SEQUENCE XLIV.

3. Cf. Luke ii. 29 et seq.
16-18. "The ceremony of consecrating and distributing
candles at the feast of the purification, and walking,
with them in the hands, in procession—whence the
names 'Candelaria,' 'Candlemas,'—probably arose from
' a desire to put Christians in remembrance of Christ, the
spiritual light, of whom Symeon did prophesy, as is read
in the church that day.' (*L'Estrange*, 'Alliance of Divine
Offices,'—c. v. Oxf. 1846 ;) in other words to illustrate
Luke ii. 32 : ' A light to lighten the Gentiles.' "—*Smith
and Cheetham's* "Dict. of Christian Antiq." vol. ii.
p. 1141.
20. The candles at the purification were made of *virgin* wax.

SEQUENCE XLV.

1 et seq. Cf. Luke i. 26-56.
29-32. Cf. Exod. iii. 2 et seq.
33-36. Cf. Numb. xvii. 8.
39, 40. "The sculptors of the middle ages often placed some
fruit in the hand of Mary to recall the fruit gathered by
Eve ; but Adam, that is to say *mankind*, may eat of the
fruit offered by the Virgin : it is the fruit of life." *Gautier*, ad loc.

SEQUENCE XLVI.

1. *Paranymphus.* The "bridesman" in Pagan marriages
was the person whose duty it was to conduct the bride
to the marriage.

SEQUENCE XLVII.

This festival commemorates the finding of the Cross,
on which our Lord suffered, by the Empress Helena,
about A.D. 326.
"Perhaps the masterpiece of Adam of St. Victor."
Neale, "Med. Hymns," page 139.

27. Cf. Gen. xxviii. 10.

30-32. "Christ therefore willed to be exalted on the Cross,
not without a reason : but that, in accordance with the
four arms of the cross, whereby the four parts of the
world be signified, He might draw all men to love, to
imitate, and to reign together with him." *Hildebert,*
quoted by *Neale,* "Med. Hymns," page 144.

36. Cf. Exod. xv. 25. "And he cried unto the Lord, and
the Lord showed him a tree, which when he had cast
into the waters, the waters were made sweet."

37,38. Cf. Exod. xvii. 6.

40-44. Cf. Exod. xii. 22, 23.

45-50. Cf. 1 Kings xvii. 10-16. "The 'two sticks' which
the widow of Sarepta was gathering, when salvation
came to her house, are expounded of the two beams,
which, by their intersection, made up the Cross." *Neale,*
"Med. Hymns," page 145.

56-60. "Fortasse sermo est de bellis sacris sive cruciatis."
Daniel, "Thes. Hymn," ii. 81. "A very clear reference
to the Crusades." *Neale,* "Med. Hymns," page 145. Cf.
Lev. xxvi. 7, 8.

61-63. When—A.D. 312—the great battle of the Milvian

bridge was imminent, about the middle of the previous afternoon Constantine saw the trophy of the Cross, figured in light, standing above the sun, and with the words "Conquer by this" attached to it. He, and the army that was with him, were seized with amazement, and he himself was in doubt as to the meaning of the appearance. As he was long considering it, night came on; and in sleep Christ appeared to him with the sign that appeared in heaven, and ordered him to make a standard of the same pattern. The next day the battle with Maxentius was fought, and the latter, while endeavouring to make his way into Rome over the bridge of boats, was lost with his whole army by the sinking of the bridge beneath them.

64-66. In the early years of the Emperor Heraclius, who reigned A.D. 610-641, Jerusalem and the supposed true Cross having been captured by the Persians, he recaptured them, A.D. 628, and brilliantly avenged the cruelties committed by Chosroes in A.D. 615.

SEQUENCE XLVIII.

5. *Patris Nostri.* St. Augustine was the second Patron-saint of the Abbey of St. Victor, and the monks there lived according to his rule.

17-20. Manichæism was most trivial in many of its points of belief, as the statement in the text would indicate.

SEQUENCE XLIX.

St. Nereus and St. Achilleus, who were brothers, are described in the "Roman Martyrology," quoted by Gautier, as having been eunuchs in the service of Flavia Domitilla, a Roman lady, in the first century, and, after having been banished with their mistress to the island of

Ponza for some years, as having suffered cruel tortures, and finally martyrdom, at Rome under the Consul Minutius Rufus, for refusing to worship idols, and abjure the true faith, into which they were said to have been baptized by St. Peter himself.

The reader will find another very interesting account of them in *Brownlow and Northcote's* "Roma Soterranea," part i. pp. 88, 120, 179-181, 185, 186; which proves them to have been soldiers in that body-guard, which the Emperor Nero generally employed to execute his cruel and bloody purposes, by an inscription to their memory, discovered in the Catacomb, or Cemetery, of Flavia Domitilla, a niece of the Emperor Vespasian, which describes them as being suddenly converted, while executing their degrading office, and, deserting the wicked camp of their leader, throwing away their weapons and accoutrements, and, confessing the faith, glorying in martyrdom for Christ's sake. The service with Flavia Domitilla—if they ever were her servants, which seems not at all certain—would be subsequent to their conversion to Christianity. The fact that they were certainly buried in the "Cœmeterium Domitillæ" at Tor Marancia, on the Via Ardentina, at Rome, would point to some connection with her to whom it belonged, but there is no reference to any in the inscription found to their memory.

The "Acts of SS. Nereus and Achilleus" state that they suffered martyrdom by the sword.

It is suggested by some authorities, that it was this St. Nereus who was saluted by St. Paul in Rom. xvi. 15. Cf. *Smith's* "Dict. of the Bible," vol. ii. page 500, Art. "Nereus."

16. Clement was one of the earliest bishops of Rome, though placed variously in order by different ancient lists.

49. Domitilla was persecuted afterwards by Aurelian, who recalled her from exile, and would have attempted her

virtue, but was struck down by God, and perished miserably. His brother, to avenge his death, set fire to the house where Domitilla was, and she perished in the flames while engaged in prayer. This is the account given in "The Golden Legend."

"Whether she really shed her blood for the faith at last is uncertain, the 'Acts of SS. Nereus and Achilleus' being of doubtful authenticity." *Brownlow and Northcote's* "Roma Soterranea," part i. pp. 120, 121.

SEQUENCE L.

This Sequence, which, from its character, could only have been intended for use in the Abbey of St. Victor, celebrates the removal thither by Hugh, afterwards of St. Victor, of a portion of the remains of St. Victor, from their first resting-place at Marseilles.

The right foot of the Saint was the relic that the Victorines of Marseilles had been induced to give up to their brethren near Paris.

St. Victor, who was a soldier, and was born at Marseilles, lived in the early part of the fourth century, and suffered martyrdom for the faith.

SEQUENCE LI.

7-12. Cf. Luke i. 19, 20.
19-24. Cf. Luke i. 57-80.
37-39. Cf. Luke i. 41-44.
40-48. Cf. John i. 29 ; i. 23; Matth. iii. 3 ; Mark, i. 3 ; Luke iii. 4 ; Isaiah xl. 3.
45. Cf. Mark i. 4, 5.
46-48. Cf. John i. 8, 9.
49-52 Cf. Matth. iii. 4 ; Mark i. 6.
54, 55. Cf. Matth. xi. 11.

SEQUENCE LII.

7. Cf. Ephesians ii. 20.
9. *Bases.* Cf. Exod. xxvi. 10 ; xxvii. 10.
Epistylia. Cf. 1 Kings vii. 6.
10. *Saga.* Cf. Exod. xxvii. 7 *et passim.*
Cortina. Cf. Exod. xxv. 1.
12. Cf. Exod. xxv. 31.
13-15. Cf. Isaiah lx. 8.
21, 22. Cf. Matth. xx. 2.
31, 32. Cf. Psalm xix. 1.
67-72. "While St. Peter and St. Paul were preaching at Rome, Nero had become passionately fond of Simon Magus, who pretended that he was the Son of God, and had performed strange prodigies before the Emperor. St. Peter came with St. Paul to the Emperor's palace, and denounced Simon to him as a demon escaped from hell. The Apostle justified his mission by striking miracles. Simon pretended at last, in order to answer him, that he could fly, and mount up to heaven. He actually threw himself off the Capitol, and supported himself in the air, but, St. Peter, having merely pronounced the name of Jesus Christ, saw Magus all at once fall down and kill himself."—*Gautier*, ad loc.

SEQUENCE LIII.

This Sequence was appointed for June 29th,—the festival of St. Peter and St. Paul,—though it really refers only to St. Peter.
2. "Primus pastor est Christus, secundus Petrus." — *Mone*, iii. 77.
13-18. Cf. Matth. iv. 18-20.
21, 22. Cf. Acts iii. 1-11.
23-26. Cf. Acts ix. 32-34.

27-29. Cf. Acts ix. 36-43.

30-32. Cf. Matth. xiv. 27-31.

33-38. Cf. Matth. xvi. 15-19 ; John vi. 68-70.

39. For Peter's denial, cf. Matth. xxvi. 69-75 ; and for his triple confession, cf. John xxi. 15-18.

42. Cf. Acts xii. 3-17.

45-48. Cf. Acts v. 14-16.

49-64. Here Adam leaves the Scripture history, and follows the " Golden Legend "—*De Sancto Petro Apostolo*— which, according to Gautier, is filled with marvels too fabulous to be reproduced.

SEQUENCE LIV.

49-54. A very difficult stanza. I am not at all sure that I have caught its drift.

61-63. Cf. Acts v. 1-11.

80. Vide note to Sequence LII. 61-72.

SEQUENCE LV.

7-10. Cf. Gen. xlix. 27.

13 *et seq.* Cf. Acts ix.

25. Cf. Acts ix. 15. " He is a chosen vessel unto me."

31. Cf. 1 Cor. i. 18. " For the preaching of the cross is to them that perish foolishness."

32, 33. Cf. 2 Cor. xi. 23-33.

40 *et seq.* Cf. 2 Cor. xii. 2-4. " I knew a man in Christ . . . such an one caught up to the third heaven, . . . and heard unspeakable words, which it is not lawful for a man to utter."

SEQUENCE LVI.

St. Margaret, one of the most popular of the martyrs of Mediæval times, was a Virgin, who suffered at the age of fifteen, under Olybrius, the prefect of Antioch in Pisidia, in the third or fourth century. Olybrius, who met her one day, as she was leading out her flock to their pasture,—for she was a shepherdess,—fell deeply in love with her, and on his suit being rejected, put her to a cruel death for her profession of Christianity. The circumstances of her martyrdom are dwelt upon in this Sequence.

49 *et seq.* This famous legend has supplied all the emblematic representations of the Saint. "It is," Mrs. Jameson remarks in her "*Sacred and Legendary Art*," vol. ii. page 517, "another form of the familiar allegory—the power of sin overcome by the power of the Cross."

SEQUENCE LVII.

St. Victor was born at Marseilles in the third century, and suffered martyrdom under Asterius, the prefect there. He had been a distinguished soldier under the Emperor Maximianus, but, having been converted to Christianity, he declined to serve any longer, and, refusing to worship idols, was put to death with horrible tortures, as related by Adam of St. Victor, in this and the following Sequences.

SEQUENCE LX.

8. Cf. Matth. iv. 21, 22.

10. Cf. Matth. xxi. 18, 19.

27, 29. Cf. Matth. xvii. 1. St. James the Greater was one of the witnesses of the Transfiguration.

30-32. Cf. Matth. xxvi. 37 ; Luke xxii. 44.

39-41. "Our Adam means here by these two wings, *preaching* and *practice.*" *Gautier*, ad loc.

42. A legendary story is told of the miraculous conversion of a magician, called Hermogenes, by St. James.

49, 50. An allusion probably to the name of "Sons of Thunder," given by our Lord to the sons of Zebedee. Cf. Mark iii. 17.

SEQUENCE LXII.

17. Cf. Matth. xvii. 1, 2.

22-24. Cf. Matth. xvii. 2. "And His face did shine as the sun."

25-27. Cf. Matth. xvii. 2. "And His raiment was white as the light."

35, 36. Cf. Luke ix. 30; Matth. xvii. 3; Mark ix. 3. "And behold there talked with Him two men, which were Moses and Elias."

38. Cf. Matth. xvii. 3.

46-48. Cf. Matth. xvii. 5; Mark ix. 6; Luke ix. 35. "While He yet spake, behold, a bright cloud overshadowed them; and behold a voice out of the cloud, which said, 'This is My beloved Son, in whom I am well pleased; hear ye Him.'"

71, 72. Cf. Matth. xvii. 6. "And when the disciples heard it, they fell on their face, and were sore afraid."

73-75. Cf. Matth. xvii. 7, 8. "And Jesus came and touched them, and said, 'Arise, and be not afraid.' And when they had lifted up their eyes, they saw no man save Jesus only."

77-81. Cf. Matth. xvii. 9. "Jesus charged them, saying, Tell the vision to no man, until the Son of Man be risen again from the dead."

SEQUENCE LXIV.

"St. Lawrence was archdeacon of Rome in the third century, and died—he is said to have been broiled to death upon a gridiron—in the persecution of Valerian. His festival was held in great honour by the Church of the Middle Ages, and himself accounted to hold a place only second to St. Stephen, in the glorious army of Martyrs." (*Durandus*, "Rational," vii. 23. Quoted by *Trench*, "Sacred Latin Poetry," page 221, *note*.)

The very great eminence attributed to St. Lawrence
is due to the simple fact, as Dr. Littledale writes to me,
that his name was prominent, as archdeacon of Rome,
in the local Roman martyrology, so as to be inserted in
the Canon of the Mass ; and, as the Roman missal made
its way over Western Europe at a date subsequent to the
disuse of the "diptichs," in which local Saints were once
commemorated everywhere in Christendom, the Saints
mentioned in the Canon of Rome were adopted just as
they stood ; and therewith St. Lawrence, marked by an
octave at Rome, took like rank, though not more
eminent than hundreds of Martyrs less distinguished
liturgically.

24. *Chely.*—"χέλυς = 'testudo,' originally the tortoise, out of
the shell of which Hermes is said to have fashioned the
first lyre." *Trench*, p. 222, *note.*

41. On the suggestion of Archbishop Trench, I have ventured
to read "cujus" for "hujus" in this line, though
Gautier has "hujus," and there would seem to be no
authority in other editions of this Sequence for the use of
"cujus."

37-42. This stanza has reference probably to the story told of
St. Lawrence by St. Ambrose in the second book of his
Offices, cap. xxviii. "Tale aurum sanctus martyr Laurentius Domino reservavit ; a quo cum quærerentur thesauri Ecclesiæ, promisit demonstraturum se. Sequenti
die pauperes duxit. Interrogatus ubi essent thesauri quos
promiserat, ostendit pauperes dicens ; hi sunt thesauri
Ecclesiæ."

43-45. *Nescit sancti nox obscurum.* "Dixit ergo Decius
Laurentio : 'aut Diis sacrificabis aut nox ista in te cum
suppliciis expandetur.' Cui Laurentius : 'mea nox obscurum non habet, sed omnia in luce clarescunt.'"
(*Golden Legend*, "de S. Laurentio martyre" sec. i., as
quoted by Gautier, ad loc.)

46. The story runs that, whilst in prison, St. Lawrence, after he had converted and baptized him, restored the sight of a certain heathen there, named Lucilius, who had become blind through weeping for his unhappy lot. In consequence of this miracle, it is further said, that many blind men came to St. Lawrence and returned with sight.

60, 61. Cf. Phil. i. 23. "Having a desire to depart and be with Christ."

62-64. Cf. Matth. x. 28. "Fear not them which kill the body, but are not able to kill the soul."

65-70. Cf. Ecclesiasticus xxvii. 5, E. V : xxvii. 6. Vulgate, "Vasa figuli probat fornax et homines justos tentatio tribulationis."

79. *Putat Rorem.* "An allusion probably to Da. iii. 50. Vulgate, 'Et fecit medium fornacis quasi ventum roris flantem.'" *Trench,* "Sac. Lat. Poetry," page 222, *note.*

SEQUENCE LXV.

43. Cf. 2 Chron. ix. 15-19. Solomon's throne is a favourite symbol of the blessed Virgin. "Salvator enim noster . . . fecit thronum, id est uterum Virginis, in quo sedet illa majestas quæ nutu concutit orbem." *Hugh of St. Victor,* quoted by Gautier, ad loc.

44. Cf. Note on Sequence 111, line 52. Judges vi. 36-40.

46. Cf. Exod. iii. 2.

55-58. Cf. Isaiah xi. i. Vide Note on Sequence ii. line 25.

69. Cf. Ezek. xliv. 2. *Porta =* "Uterus Virginis."

SEQUENCE LXVI.

50. Hugh of St. Victor, as quoted by Gautier on this passage, gives the following explanation of "*vitis*" and "*oliva,*" as synonyms of the Virgin :

"*Vitis* florendo fructificat et ejus fructus inebriat ;

sic Beata Maria per florem suæ virginitatis fructificavit Christum, botrum nostræ redemptionis, qui suos electos inebriat in mundo vino gratiæ, in cœlo vino gloriæ."— *Sermon* 55.

"*Oliva* figurat misericordiam : fuit ergo Beata Maria oliva per misericordiam, et tanto pretiosior per misericordiam quanto excellentior per gratiam."—*Sermon* 47.

SEQUENCE LXVII.

St. Bartholomew the Apostle is said to have preached the Gospel in India, meaning thereby probably Arabia Felix, which was sometimes called India by the ancients. Some allot Armenia to him as his mission-field.

Gautier quotes largely from the *Golden Legend* "de S. Bartholomaeo," sec i., in illustration of the narration of the Apostle's wonder-works contained in this Sequence; but Adam has apparently followed the legend so closely as to render unnecessary any further or fuller account of the various incidents.

The reader will also find a full account of the legend in *Ordericus Vitalis*, "Eccl. Hist. of England and Normandy," bk. ii., cap. ix.

20. *Berith.* Cf. Judges vii. 33 ; ix. 4, where this demon is called "Baal-Berith."

25-28. Tradition says that St. Bartholomew caused a devil to come out of a certain man, named Pseustius, and that the king of the country, hearing of it, asked him to cure his daughter, who was a lunatic, which the Apostle proceeded to do.

SEQUENCE LXVIII.

1. *Æterni festi* is Gautier's text, but I am bound to say that many others read *interni*, and among them Neale,

who says—"*Mediæval Hymns,*" page 133, "I understand the poet to mean that the external celebration of the festival is only the outspoken expression of the internal joy of the heart."

SEQUENCE LXX.

7-9. These lines refer to the twofold celebration of St. John the Baptist in the Church's year, viz., his birth on the 24th of June, and his beheading on the 20th of August.
21-24. Cf. Matth. iii. 7, 8 ; Luke iii. 7.
25-30. Cf. Luke vi. 17, 18 ; Matth. xiv. 1-13.
37. Cf. Mark vi. 21.
28-42. Cf. Mark vi. 23-29.
43. Cf. John iii, 30. "He must increase, but I must decrease."

SEQUENCE LXXI.

Much confusion and more fable enters into the history of St. Giles. He is said to have been a Greek, born at Athens in the sixth or seventh century—for even on this point the accounts of him differ—who migrated to France in order to secure a greater seclusion from the haunts of men than he could hope for in the more populous districts of his native country. Settling in a hermitage—first in one of the deserts near the mouth of the Rhone, finally in a forest in the diocese of Nismes, he gave himself to solitude and heavenly meditation with such entire devotion of spirit as raised him to the highest reputation. Having been traced to his place of retirement, as related in Adam's Sequences, by the king of the country, he was prevailed upon to establish a little monastic fraternity, which in time grew to be a regular Benedictine monastery, and was surrounded by a town taking its name from the saint.

28-30. This miracle is said in another Sequence upon St Giles, which is given at length in *Mone*, vol. iii. page 165, to have been performed at Arles on the daughter of one Theocrita, who had been long ill of a severe fever.

56-60. This is a most difficult stanza. "The intention," Dr. Littledale writes to me, "is that every one who prays to Giles will be as successful in his petitions as the king was, who obtained pardon at the saint's intercession, and that such is the witness of Gaul. There *may* be a reference to some prayer of the king's, like Solomon's, that petitions should always be heard, as he himself had been." Gautier is quite silent on the passage. The king, to whom the whole stanza alludes, was probably Charles Martel, to whom St. Giles is said to have been sent on a mission by his bishop.

SEQUENCE LXXIII.

13. Cf. Ezek. xliv. 1-3 ; Cant. iv. 15.

16-18. Cf. Ecclesiasticus xxiv. 15.

22-24. Cf. Ecclesiasticus xxiv. 14.

37-42. Cf. 1 Chron. ix. 17-19.

57. As Adam of St. Victor was writing this stanza, the story goes, the crypt, where he was, was suddenly filled with light, and he saw the Virgin, smiling and inclining her head towards him. The miracle was commemorated by a chapel being erected on the spot, and a representation carved upon its walls of the poet upon his knees, looking up at the Virgin.

Mater Pietatis. Cf. Ecclesiasticus xxiv. 18.

SEQUENCE LXXIV.

3. *Luminosis Cordibus.* "Corda in festo luminum dicuntur luminosa." *Daniel,* "Thes. Hymn," vol. v. page 240, *note.*

II.   S

21. *Compunctiva*—A difficult word, especially in its application here, if I have translated it rightly. It does not appear in any dictionary to which I have had access ; neither Daniel nor Gautier notice it ; and the old fifteenth century French translation, which the latter appends of the whole Sequence, simply reproduces it as "*compunctive.*" Upon Dr. Littledale's suggestion, who says that he has little doubt upon the subject, I have taken it to be the same as *Dolorosa*, "having regard to the ecclesiastical use of '*compungor*' = '*Dolore afficior ;*' '*Anxius sum ;*' and that there is a reference to the office 'De Compassione Mariæ Virginis ';' or it may allude to the interpretation of the name 'Mary' or 'Mariam '= *Miriam*, which is often given, viz., '*bitterness of the sea.*'"

"The Jews say that the sister of Moses was so named from *bitterness*, because at that time the Egyptians made the lives of the sons of Israel bitter. It was a name which was afterwards to be held in great reverence and honour, for it is *the same as Mary*, the name of our Lord's blessed mother." Canon W. R. Churton's *Note* on Exod. xv. 20, in S. P. C. K. '*Comm. on O. Test.,*' 1876.

Cf. also 23rd verse—*Marah ;*—and Ruth i. 20—*Mara*.

27-29. Cf. Exod. iii. 2.

33-34. Cf. Cant. iv. 12. "A garden inclosed is my sister, my spouse ; a spring shut up, a fountain sealed."

43, 44. Isaiah xlv. 8. "Let the earth open, and let them bring forth salvation," &c.

45-47. *Mons.* Cf. Daniel, ii. 34. The idea being that the stone, that "was cut without hands," signifies Jesus, and the mountain, from which it proceeded, the Blessed Virgin.

Castellum. "Virgo Maria . . est *castrum* securitate, Murus vel *turris* fortitudine." *Hugh of St. Victor,* "Serm." 34.

Aula and *thalamus*. Cf. Psalm xix. 5, *Vulgate*. "Et ipse tanquam sponsus procedens de thalamo suo." So in St. Ambrose's beautiful hymn, "Veni, Redemptor gentium."

> "Procedit e *thalamo* suo,
> Pudoris *aula* regia.
> Geminæ gigas substantiæ."

Templum. Mary is so called, as having contained God in her womb.

Civitas. Cf. Psalm lxxxvii. 3. "Gloriosa dicta sunt de te, *Civitas* Dei."

Sequence LXXV.

19-30. Cf. Gen. iii. 15. "I will put emnity between thee and the woman, and between thy seed and her seed ; it shall bruise thy head, and thou shalt bruise his heel."

INDEX OF FIRST LINES OF THE
SECOND VOLUME.

LATIN.

INDEX OF FIRST LINES OF THE SECOND VOLUME.

ENGLISH.

END OF VOL. II.

www.ingramcontent.com/pod-product-compliance
Lightning Source LLC
Chambersburg PA
CBHW030352270326
41926CB00009B/1066

*9 7 8 3 3 3 7 7 7 8 1 3 2 *